Charlie's Thoughts

Charlie's Thoughts

By Charles Butland
Internationally renowned inventor/entrepreneur

Original Musical Soundtrack Included

Produced by Heidi Magleby Olsen for Signature Music, Inc.
Executive Producer: Charlie Butland

Foreword by Barry Spilchuk
Story adaptations by Susan Evans McCloud

FIRST EDITION

Edited by Tara Chappell, Cynthia Spillman, Kellene Ricks Adams,
    and Ellyn Clifton
Cover design by Perry Van Schelt
Photography by Martin van Hemert

Library of Congress Catalog Card Number: 98-75811
ISBN 0-9657536-2-X

Musical soundtrack produced by Heidi Magleby Olsen
Executive Producer: Charles Butland
For Signature Music, Inc. All rights reserved.

Published by Signature Publishing
United States of America
www.signaturepublishing.net

DEDICATION

This book is dedicated to the loving memory of my mother, Mary Wilson Butland, and to the hundreds of people who have appeared in my "movie of life" and have made the experience worth writing about.

I also dedicate this book to Heidi Magleby Olsen, whose talents made the musical concept possible. She molded an original historical soundtrack to *Charlie's Thoughts* by producing, directing, writing, and singing the beautiful songs, blending words and harmony for each chapter's themes. It was amazing watching her creativity at work in the recording studio: one hand on the control, one hand around her small child, and a phone to her ear. She was always pleasant, loving, and graceful, characteristics reflected in her beautiful music.

I would also like to dedicate this book to my adopted daughter, Ensie, and to her brother, Ali Abedi, who at age 17 was tragically killed on Halloween night, 1998, while saving five lives in a burning disco in Sweden.

Finally, I dedicate this book to the future inventors and entrepreneurs who will open up new frontiers, much like the early settlers did coming West, to make this world a better place in which to live.

Charles Butland

The soundtrack is dedicated to

Charles Taylor,

Tanner Magleby,

and Sydney Marie,

because everything I do is for you.

HMO

FOREWORD

Imagine walking into your favorite restaurant for a quick bite to eat. All the tables are empty except for one in the corner, where an enthusiastic group sits. As you sit down, a friendly voice calls out, "Why don't you join us?" You hesitate for a moment, but then think, *Oh well, they seem nice enough. Why not?*

As you take your place at the empty seat, the gentleman who called out your name says, "Welcome! Let me introduce you to my friends!"

As the introductions progress, you are genuinely impressed, shocked, and amazed at who is present. The first person on your left is none other than Thomas Edison, the wonderful inventor. Next is Aristotle, the famous thinker from years gone by. To his left is the renowned, thought-provoking humorist, Will Rogers. Donald Trump is introduced next as the modern-day entrepreneur and risk-taker and—for a dash of humor—one of America's favorite funny men, Henny Youngman.

The only one left unannounced is the gentleman who welcomed you. "Who are you?" you ask, but before he can answer, Donald Trump blurts out, "Oh, he is all of us!" A bit confused, you ask for clarification, and Mr. Trump continues: "A while ago people started to wonder what would happen if you could combine all the thoughts, creativity, energy, wisdom, guts, and humor of this magnificent group of men. Well, we thought about it, and we decided that we needed a spokesperson to represent us. All of us!"

You begin to realize that this friendly mystery man is uniquely special. "We found the perfect match," Mr. Trump continues. "Someone who represents all of us. Say hello to Mr. Charles Butland!"

In your imagination, Charles Butland invited you to join him at a table. In actuality, he is extending that same invitation to be with him through these pages. You will enjoy getting to know Charlie. He truly is a composite of all the above-mentioned gentleman. . . and more!

If you take the first initial from a name of each of our celebrity guests—H from Henny, E from Edison, A from Aristotle, R from Rogers, and T from Trump—you get

HEART. That is what makes the book you are about to read different from any other books you may have read about inventors and creative personalities. You will not only find out about what goes on in the mind of this gentle genius, you will also discover what is in his heart and soul.

Charles Butland has been a mentor, a tutor, and an inspiration to many people. After reading his story, I am sure you will add your name to the list of his many fans. Enjoy!

Respectfully,

Barry Spilchuk, coauthor

A Cup of Chicken Soup for the Soul

PREFACE

When I came up with the idea of writing a book someone amusingly stated, "Charlie, if you are going to write a book you have to *read* one first." That inference might have stopped a lot of people, but it's the very thing that motivates me.

I had no scientific background enabling me to envision and create any of my inventions, but that never stopped me. I'm like the bumblebee that flies despite the fact that every single aerodynamic probability dictates that he can't. The bumblebee doesn't know he can't fly, so he does. I don't know I can't invent—or write—so I do. I try to show by example that there are no limitations on people who believe in themselves.

When I set out to invent something, I think and feel with my body, not my head. I know I am the thinker of the thought, not the thought itself. This comes from another source that seems to come through me with the right answers. I simply empower these thoughts with passion and action until they take a physical form. After experiencing this a few times, you begin to realize that you can create anything.

As with everything I do, I wanted this book to stand out. So, with the help of many people, we created a soundtrack for each chapter, a new invention to make books more entertaining. I want to thank those people.

First, thanks to the entire staff of Counterpoint Studios in Salt Lake City, a state-of-the-art facility that made the musical recordings literally come to life. Thanks also to the musicians, vocalists, and engineers involved: Kurt Bestor, Lex de Azevedo, Sam Cardon, Michael McLean, Heidi Magleby Olsen, Michael Pedersen, Windslow Farr, Richard "Sneez" Senese, Vince Frates, Craig Poole, Jenell Slack, Brett Raymond, Joslyn Petty, Guy Roberts, Brett Manning, Cinde Borup, Rick and Curt Goad, Rick Hancey, Howard Blake, Bob Abeyta, Blair Sutherland, Susie, Johnny, Jake, and Signature Music Incorporated.

A special thanks to Mr. Joe Barbera for his friendship and contributions and to Vincent Molina for his coaching and expertise, not only in the publishing and printing industry, but in the "plussing" area as well. Thanks to Susan Evans McCloud for her beautifully creative contributions and additions. Martin van Hemert and Perry Van Schelt deserve recognition for the photography and photo illustration for the cover of the book and CD. Tim Doot at Pinnacle Music and Elaine Petersen made extremely helpful suggestions. Many more people gave countless hours of moral, emotional, and spiritual support: Dale and Pamela Magleby for opening their doors and always being on call; Tara Chappell and Cynthia Spillman for their gift in editing; a very big thanks for Kellene Ricks Adams for her long days and nights in the final stages of the book; Ellyn Clifton for taking the time to review the book and for her continued support and encouragement during the entire creative process; and, of course, Ensie.

Barry Spilchuk is amazing to say the least. His time and encouragement will always be remembered and his lifelong friendship always treasured. Thanks also to the 10,000 Income Builders Forum graduates; the forum is the vehicle by which the entire vision and creativity for this project was born. Thanks especially to Bernie, Lynn, and Tony Dohrmann for their enduring friendship and for the amazing gift of IBI.

I strive to see the invisible, touch the intangible, and create the impossible; so can you! Enjoy your journey through *Charlie's Thoughts*, and I'll see you in your next dream.

Charles Butland

INTRODUCTION

As human beings, in the midst of our own personal struggle to master ourselves and triumph over the trials that beset us, we are drawn to the stories of those who have risen from extreme suffering and hardship to ascend and overcome. Charlie Butland is a powerful, unique example of one of these.

Though his successes and achievements are, in themselves, impressive, his real power comes from the insights and perceptions he has garnered along the way. It is these he shares in boldly drawn stories, in snatches of wisdom and pathos, to astound, uplift, and encourage the reader. He explains us to ourselves through personal examples of what he has learned about himself, human nature, and life. His dynamic, yet gentle, spirit comes through in all that he says, making us feel we have touched not only the feelings and thoughts, but the man.

Charlie raises a refreshing voice of hope and faith amid today's skeptical wilderness of disillusionment and despair. He encourages those precious, yet outdated, virtues that served for generations before us, proving by his own experiences how powerful their force can still be. Man was made, Charlie maintains, to create his own world, master himself, and experience the joy that comes only when we seek aid from a Higher Source, thereby discovering and unlocking the best within ourselves.

"One moment in a man's life," Emerson wrote, "is a fact so stupendous as to take the luster from all fiction." In this one man's life, we are drawn to the magnificence of the human spirit and encouraged to exercise our own powers, welcome the challenge, believe, and succeed!

Susan Evans McCloud

Charlie's Thoughts

Table of Contents

Prelude Song
Victory in the Night

By Michael Pedersen

Instrumental

Childhood and Innocence
Prayer of the Children

Written and performed by Kurt Bestor

Can you hear the prayer of the children
On bended knee in the shadow of an unknown room?
Empty eyes with no more tears to cry
Turning heavenward toward the light.
Cry, "Jesus help me to see the morning light
Of one more day.
But if I should die before I wake
I pray my soul to take."

Can you feel the hearts of the children
Aching for home, for something of their very own?
Reaching hands with nothing to hold on to
But hope for a better day, a better day.

Cry, "Jesus help me to feel the love again
In my own land.
But if unknown roads lead away from home
Give me loving arms, away from harm!"

Can you hear the voice of the children
Softly pleading for silence in a shattered world?
Angry guns preach a gospel full of hate
The blood of the innocent on their hands.

Cry, "Jesus, help me to feel the sun again
On my face.
For when darkness clears I know you're near
Bringing peace again."

Can you hear the prayer of the children?

GROWING UP
WITH
CHARLIE

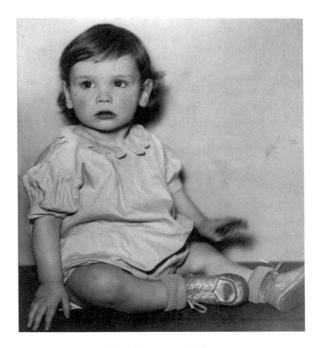

Charlie as an infant

"It's good to be great, but it's greater to be good."

GROWING UP WITH CHARLIE

Recently I made a commitment to myself that I would write a book about my adventurous thinking, thinking that created experiences which enabled me to define my reality and helped me to rediscover myself as an inventor in this world. With everything I do, I am motivated by a Higher Power that seems to guide me along life's path. I believe this power talks to me daily, communicating with me in countless ways, though I am not always listening.

As a child, I was always aware of something larger in my life, something beyond the understanding of my hulking father who terrorized me most of my preadolescent years.

I used to wake up in the mornings full of joy, a joy I could not describe in words. But I knew it was far beyond what we term "happy" in the everyday sense of the word.

I spent most of my young life, between the ages of seven and thirteen, exploring nature in the woods or meadows with my faithful dog, Prince. This pattern might have been, in part, an escape from the home, where much of the time I experienced real terror. I believe it was something beyond that, however, and this Power, which I found in nature and cannot comprehend nor define, lures me to this day.

A SPARTAN EXISTENCE

It is important for me to point out that I believe my parents did the best they could under the circumstances, considering their own backgrounds and the ways in which they had been raised. My father was a half-breed American Indian who came from the Blackfoot-Minioc tribe in Maine. He was raised by a brutal mother whom everyone feared, including her husband.

My father knew no other behavior to model, except what he had learned at home from his parents. When his kids were out of line, he did not think twice about enforcing his opinions and anger with beatings. He degraded us continually to help reinforce our shame-based image and the constant feelings that we were never enough and would probably not amount to anything in life.

When you start out with these kinds of insecurities, it may take your whole lifetime to overcome them. My three older brothers experienced the same treatment and had much difficulty later in life because of it.

My mother came from an unusual background as well. Her Scottish forebears settled a little island above northeast Canada, which you could only reach by ferry. Her ancestors were used to hard living and to sharing with the Indians who were native to that part of the land.

My mother's mother died when Mother was thirteen or fourteen years old, and so she took upon herself much of the responsibility for raising and feeding her brothers and sisters; she possessed excellent skills as a cook. Marriage to my father must have been little more than a continuation of this spartan existence of discipline and self-denial she had carved out for herself as a girl.

THE PERFECT NORMAN ROCKWELL PAINTING

I made my first move to run away from home when I was four years old. My mother had me tied to a clothesline in the front yard, much like you would tie up a dog. It didn't take me long to figure out how to get out of the harness and split down the road, naked as a jaybird!

I had my first ride in a police car when an officer brought me home—and it was not the last. Of course, my parents had no idea why I was running away and inflicted more abuse on me, in the form of a beating, to teach me a lesson.

Even though I was only four, I felt my life was in danger. When you are raised in that kind of fear, you do one of two things: you cave in and become very submissive or you try to hang on to your sanity and sense of belonging. I found that peace, that sense of being and belonging, even a sense of harmony, in the woods. As I took long hikes, nature worked upon my senses, healing the less visible wounds and even restoring some sort of inner harmony within my confused young spirit. I was fortunate that we lived in a small rural community in Massachusetts, bordering New Hampshire, where the beautiful outdoors were all around me when I was in need.

I spent a lot of time by myself, sometimes going fishing at a local river or pond. It looked like a perfect Norman Rockwell painting: a little boy wearing old clothes and shoes with worn-out soles that flapped when he walked. I carried a can of worms that were crawling over the top of the can, a stick for a fishing pole with a kite string tightly wrapped at the end, and a hook I stole from my father that he used for sea fishing. The hook was so large it could have been used to snag a tuna, but it wasn't very suitable for the small fish I was after at Clark's Pond.

It didn't matter much, because when I got to my favorite hideout, I felt surrounded by love and freedom. There was no one who could beat, frighten, or demean me. I loved it. Nature and my faithful dog Prince—that's all I needed.

I am sure I did not entirely realize that I was finding ways to compensate for the lack of sympathy and understanding, the lack of love I experienced at home. My hideout became the breeding ground for my creative thinking, which carried me throughout my life.

THE TRUTH WILL GET YOU BEATEN

I used to lie a lot because nothing that meant anything was real or understandable to me. At first, I told my parents the truth, that I had complied with their trivial restrictions and demands. But they always claimed I was lying and punished me anyway. *Well,* my childish mind reasoned, *if that is what truth is about, I will lie to get what I want.*

I did this for many years, not in defiance or out of immoral choice, but largely as a deliberate, sometimes unconscious, effort to survive. You hear a lot about the beautiful concept that "the truth will set you free."

During my tumultuous youth, it did just the opposite. My interpretation was that truth would get you abused and beaten, and little else.

To gain attention and sympathy for myself, I would go to my girlfriend's home. I was only a lad of six at the time. I would tell her mom that I had nothing to eat because my mother walked out of the house to go to Boston and left us with no food. This solution was effective but short-term. I say short-term because my girlfriend's parents called the school and told them of my plight, which was really only a figment of my imagination. There was, however, nothing imaginary about the beating I got for starting the terrible rumor. There was no doubt in my parents' minds that I was a troubled child, but they couldn't accept the responsibility that they may have caused this state. They were incapable of looking to themselves for answers, for their own lack of mature, consistent behavior.

I spent all the time I could away from home and dreamed of the day I would be free from these captors. The positive aspect of this seemingly grim situation was that it enabled me to develop an unusual independence and fueled my creative juices in deep, vital ways. I began to create my own reality, which allowed me the ability to cope with the cruel restrictions I was under at home.

I became quite proficient in selling things because I possessed this great imagination and an amazing amount of enthusiasm. I sold everything I could get my hands on, including things that didn't belong to me, like my father's electrical supplies (he was an electrician). The stuff was just lying around, and I thought it was junk. At that age and with my imagination, anything around me was fair game.

As I got a bit older, I sent away for shoes, raffle tickets, and all sorts of trivial products to sell. I even peddled eggs from our own hen coop door-to-door. Nothing was beyond me. I would try anything to create ways to make money, anything to create imagery—real enough and powerful enough—to keep me from the terror I felt. I did everything I could to stay away from home, because once I was there, it turned into a prison for me.

One day, a man carrying what looked like a one-quart ice cream box with a red cross on it came to our door. My father stuck some money in a slot at the top of the box. *That looks pretty easy,* I thought, and went in search of an ice cream box. When I found one, I drew a red cross on it with my mother's lipstick and headed off on my new money-making venture. Not many people were fooled, and I soon had my second

ride home in a police car. I was only five years old at
the time and had no idea that what I was doing was
wrong until I arrived home. I simply thought I'd found
another great idea to make money.

I was not allowed out of the house during the week-
days, except to go to school. Even in high school, I
could only go out on weekends with strict curfews. It
was then that I used my cunning ways to fake illness
and, after making a perfectly believable dummy to
place in my bed, I would crawl out the second-story
window to play with my friends. The only setback was
the horror I experienced when, at last, I sneaked back.
Every time I watched movies of people in prison
breaks, I would tremble inside because I was able to
identify with them vividly.

THE VITAL PERCEPTION

The reality of it, as I understand myself today, is
that this was the self-imposed, self-constructed life I
chose so I could learn more about who I really am. I
might not have been able to expand my innate powers
had I not been challenged in this way. I might not have
thought in the creative manner I did in order to survive
if I had not experienced the drama of my early childhood. Now, I can look at it heroically, rather than

painfully. My parents played the perfect, or at least necessary, part in my life's movie, which actually contributed in propelling me to greater heights. I now realize and firmly believe that all experiences, good or bad, possess the power to have only a positive value in one's life.

If your thinking is correct, you realize that **events** have nothing to do with your reality. Your **perception of the events** is the vital, overriding factor in all things. Herein lies the real freedom, which I had no conception of when I was a child. I had been inventing things since I was five years old, but at that age, it was impossible to possess the ability to recognize the value of inventions or perceptions.

When I was five, I was sent to a local store to buy soap powder. I remember watching the clerk pull the soap off the fourth shelf with a long pole. *Why couldn't they have a machine with a picture of the product in the window and, when you push a button, the product falls out,* I wondered. I didn't know it then, but I had conceptualized in my young mind the future vending machine. Had I lived in an environment of credibility, with a proper belief system in place, I could have moved forward with this idea, regardless of my age.

During the next few years, I mentally developed a visual phone that enabled you to see the person you were talking to, a computer that would think like our brain, spaceships that would fly to the moon, and many more wonders and achievements that have already arrived on the scene. The one vision I had at age seven was a car that could travel to any city or place without the driver having to steer. You could press a button on the dash and magically be driven to your destination by an electronic or magnetic devise imbedded in the road that propelled the car. I even thought of collision avoidance systems that would protect the driver.

In 1997, in San Diego, I saw my vision being demonstrated along a five-mile course that was specifically constructed to drive these cars by magnets imbedded in the highway, and it worked successfully. If implemented, this could mean faster, safer driving without the use of fossil fuels.

All this teeming, creative energy within me was born from necessity and affliction. I developed the priceless qualities of ingenuity and self-reliance. I knew what it meant to appreciate beauty in contrast to that which was unsightly and degrading in my life. I acquired the rare gift of being able to carry one's happiness and one's purpose inside. I was learning my lessons early. I didn't have time to dwell on things that would hold me back; I had this tremendous energy and enthusiasm, along with a great desire to taste life — all of it.

LEAVING GREEN PASTURES

Gratefully, my childhood was not "normal." Children deserve a time of innocence and freedom. Watching children frolicking about is like experiencing nature in its purest form. They radiate innocence with unrestricted thought patterns and freely perceive the new world around them, full of love and guilelessness, without judgment or limitations. They fear nothing because they come from a place of love that knows no apprehension, mistrust, or other restrictions. Their life is all play, as it should be with each of us.

Somehow, these innocent children left beautiful green pastures to come to a new dimension in life that would change their existence forever. They entered a world of opinion, intellect, and rigidity. They exchanged true contact with a Higher Power for contact with the human race. To belong, they had to give up their innocence in order to enter into a vastly different sphere that would restructure the very core of their thinking and perception. Love and acceptance became conditional. The child's reality was redefined to follow finite, ever-shifting tribal customs and beliefs.

Children start to develop sadness when they feel separated from a place of play and innocence, from the love and warmth of the womb of Spirit and of their Higher Power. They are accustomed to a place where they feel safe and connected, but they become redefined so they can survive in the mainstream of their new life as members of this race we call Human. Void of conscious memories of their past lives, children enter a new world to shape their destiny, to recreate that loving flower of God again.

I view my childhood as heroic. I can only feel proud of my stand never to lose sight of that sweetness within, that violet light of eternity, the goodness that tumbled upon me with the softness of new snow-flakes—an essence or power lying just above the illusionary sphere I was living in, just above the oscillations of the mind-set of this physical world. Through all the turmoil of rejection and physical abuse, I never lost sight of that sweetness and joy that spread like a quiet, protective layer above my head, above the shadows through which I walked. I always felt there was an overwhelming sense of warmth, love, and freedom waiting for me when I found my way back Home.

CHARLIE'S THOUGHTS
ON CHILDHOOD AND INNOCENCE

It's good to be great, but it's greater to be good.

• • •

There is no legacy so rich as honesty,
and honesty will always set you free.

• • •

The best part of my childhood is that it is over.

• • •

If you are honest because honesty is the best policy,
then your honesty is corrupt.
Being honest doesn't need a decision based on policy.
It is a natural part of you.

• • •

If you are ever doing
something wrong,

your insides have a way
of communicating that to you.

• • •

Lies are the collapse of an alibi system.
It binds you up, and you lose some freedom.
Truth will always set you free.

• • •

We're so different, except we're so much alike.

• • •

He who laughs, lasts. With all the holes in our body,
we can't take ourselves too seriously. There is humor
in almost everything in life if one views life
in a humorous manner. Humor and laughter
are chemically and physically good for you.

• • •

Humility is not submissive weakness
but rather a submissive respect.

• • •

Humility is when you change force feeding
into nourishment for the soul.

• • •

15

Calmness is a controlled condition
of your internal vibrant force.
When you are at peace with yourself,
there is no turbulence,
which allows a universal power
to radiate your soul.

• • •

When you have no demands on you,
everything is available to you.

• • •

When you were born, you cried and the world rejoiced.
When you die, the world cries and you rejoice.

• • •

Dreams and Goals
The Boy's Got a Dream

Performed by Brett Raymond and Heidi Magleby Olsen

He wakes up in the mornin', responds to the light of day.
All he's ever known is all work and no play,
But he's always had a vision, he's always had a goal,
And never has he wavered from the things that he's been told.

The boy's got a dream, and on his face is showin'
He's a boy on the move, he knows where he's goin'.
He knows what has to be done, from the challenge he will not run.
You can tell by the look in his eyes, the boy's got a dream.

Every night before she goes to sleep she gets down on her knees
And she prays to the Father that her dreams she'll always keep.
She's heard her call, she'll give her all to be all she can be
'Cause she knows all things are possible to every girl whose got a
    dream.

The girl's got a dream and on her face is showin'
She's a girl on the move, she knows where she's goin'.
She knows what has to be done, from the challenge she will not
    run.
You can tell by the look in her eyes, the girl's got a dream.

The day the two got married and they became a team
Life is so much better now 'cause now they share a dream.
And he's become her hero, and she's become his queen.
There's nothing like a family that together share a dream.

And they got a dream, and on their face is showin'
They're a family that's on the move, they know where they're
    goin'.
They know what has to be done, and together the race they will
    run.
You can tell by the look in their eyes
And they got a dream. . . they've got a dream.

SCHOOL
DAYS

School days, Charlie (age 19)

"Dreams are the spiritual DNA of your soul,
the blueprint of your ultimate achievement."

School Days

My first dream was to *be* somebody or create something important that I could use to blanket all the negative programming I had learned growing up. I had to create a new identity for myself because I felt flawed.

My high school and early college days were the very best years of my life. I was a muscular 195-lb. kid who excelled in sports, especially football. I found out, unconsciously, that I could take out my hostilities on my opponent. The rougher it got, the better I liked it. I was one of the best fullbacks in the state, but suddenly, my dream of becoming a college football star seemed to be shattered when I was thrown out of high school for a regrettable altercation with my gym teacher.

During the spring and summer following my dismissal, I worked in the hull of a ship wrapping large cable around the inside of a tank for twelve hours a day, seven days a week. Still in pursuit of my dream, I applied to Bridgeton Academy in Maine, a prep school that would launch me into college. I was accepted and had saved enough money to pay for my own tuition.

This time, I controlled my aggressive behavior, graduated with honors, and contributed to one of Bridgeton Academy's best football records in history up to that time.

NO DEAD-END KID

My dream started to come into focus again as numerous colleges around the country began recruiting me. (For every college that wanted me, however, there were fifty professors who didn't! But that didn't stop me.) I wanted to stay close to my home town so I would remain in the range of the local media, in hopes that they would continue following my career and stroking my ego.

I accepted a four-year scholarship to Boston University that covered everything from tuition to books and board. I became the starting fullback for a prestigious college that was playing major teams like Army, Navy, and Penn State. I had arrived!

I knew how to work hard, and now I had good reasons for putting my childish ways behind me and giving my best. I had come from behind, climbed all the hills, and claimed my dream. For the first time in my memory, I felt proud as a person, recognizing the accomplishments I had achieved through adversity. I recall a writer in high school who described me as a "scholastic misfit and candidate for the 'Dead-End Kids.'" He may have been right then, but I had become something different. My image of myself had altered because how I felt inside had significantly changed. For the first time, I could enjoy looking at myself: I could trust myself. I dared to keep making more plans and dreaming new dreams. I knew I had triumphed when, through my efforts, my first dream to be somebody was realized. I knew there would be many more triumphs to come.

A BLUEPRINT FOR ACHIEVEMENTS

Dreams are the spiritual DNA of your soul, the blueprint of your ultimate achievements. Nothing in this world exists without dreaming and desiring it first. Even this writing is a dream I had. I felt I had experienced life and its emotions to their fullest extent: success and failure, love and hate, wealth and poverty, health and sickness, joy and depression, giving and taking, happiness and sadness, fear and courage. I have experienced many dimensions of these and am a better person because of it. With each hardship overcome, each challenge faced, each sorrow or difficulty surmounted, I have become more thoughtful and sensitive, more caring, and truly stronger.

Experiences such as these can only be learned through living them. You can't have your computer describe a sunset, but you can feel the warm glow of a sinking sun that comes after successfully meeting the day's challenge you set for yourself. You can intellectually know all the wisdom of the world, what has been expressed and achieved by others, but unless you experience it personally, the true wisdom, the power and purity of it, will forever elude you.

What I bring to the world is the ability to manipulate energy from an invisible life force and shape it into a reality. This Life Source is the multicolored, multifaceted tapestry from which we mold our future. It is flexible, nondimensional, unconfined. Therefore, we can mold it to fit any pattern that our own skills, imagination, or desire can contrive.

If you would like to see this power in action, watch children at play. They live in a nondimensional world, uncluttered by rigid belief systems and restrictions adults place on themselves. This quality, difficult to pinpoint or define, is the most creative element of a growing soul. It needs to be nourished and loved unconditionally, not judged or based upon an unthinking endorsement of the belief system of parents or society.

It is at this inner point that each beautiful, pure soul needs love and self-esteem in order to become the best it can be, to fulfill the highest measure of its own being—a true child of God. A dream. Each dream is a fragment of this innocent state, a firm stepping-stone toward the realization of self, the flowering of self into this powerful ideal that every child of God, struggling through the mortal experience, has a right to attain.

CHARLIE'S THOUGHTS ON DREAMS AND GOALS

Dreams are the spiritual DNA of our souls,
the blueprints of our ultimate achievements.

• • •

An idea is just a thought
until a will is put into action.

• • •

I move today,
from what I was yesterday,
to who I am.

• • •

What we are is God's gift to us;
what we become is our gift to God.
Our gift of life is that
He gave us free will.
What we do with these choices

are directly proportionate
to the gifts we give ourselves.

• • •

Things are not what they seem,
they are what they are.
Every thought has its own reality.
I see the invisible.
I touch the intangible.
I achieve the impossible.
Some things seem unreal,
yet they become real by belief.

• • •

If you have no goals,
there are no roads to get there.

• • •

An unaimed arrow never misses its target.

• • •

A mind-set of success does not recognize
obstacles that interfere with goals.

• • •

You don't have to be the biggest, brightest person
in the world, you just need to think you are.

• • •

Thoughts create images,
feelings create desire,
desires create goals.

• • •

To measure a man,
measure his heart and his goals.

• • •

My past is a reference book for my future.
I am what I am,
and what I am is beautiful, strong, and free.

• • •

You will never make more
than you think you can,
and you will never keep more
than you think you deserve.

• • •

You never see obstacles until you take
your eyes off the goal.

• • •

Don't think about goals, think about paths.

• • •

I am the difference.

• • •

There is nothing stronger in the human mind
than an idea whose time has come.
It becomes burned into one's psyche
like obsessions until it has been
brought to reality.

• • •

There are no right or wrong choices,
only consequences.

• • •

Ultimately, you have no choice
but to feel what you are feeling.
You can never hide feelings.
Feelings are real. Words are symbols.

28

*It is important to have good communication
with yourself and understand yourself
from your deepest level.
Your feelings will ultimately
show you what you are.*

• • •

*Expectations are extractions of a
rhythm from past events to fit
into a framework for the future.*

• • •

*Goals and paths are not necessarily
the same thing. If you center only
on your goal, you are missing
valuable lessons, and life will
move away from you.*

• • •

*Self-interest is not the same as selfish behavior.
When someone acts in self-interest, he does so
for personal growth, without infringing
on someone else. A person behaving selfishly
infringes on others in order to get
what he or she wants.*

• • •

Instead of waiting for your ship to come in,
go build one!

• • •

Knowing others is intelligence.
Knowing yourself is wisdom.
Helping to mold others is strength.
Mastering yourself is true power.

• • •

Nothing in this life is guaranteed,
and it doesn't have to be.

• • •

When you water your conscious mind,
seeds of affirming thoughts take root
and the roses bloom.

• • •

If you don't have what you want,
you are not committed 100 percent.
You have to think, do, and dream of your goals
day and night until they become reality
in a physical form.
Every thought has it's own reality
to bring it into the physical realm.

• • •

*Standard is a predictable behavior
void of creative direction.*

• • •

Imagination is the first step to actualization.

• • •

*The day you think you have arrived
is the day you are actually leaving.
We are never a finished product,
only a potential of someone we want to be.*

• • •

A penny saved is worthless.

• • •

*Don't listen to echoes of the past.
They are gone forever and can only take you
back to trails of darkness going nowhere.*

• • •

*I am never a finished product,
only a future potential of what I'm becoming.*

• • •

In Loving Memory of Cinde Borup
Composer of *There Is a Place*

Fear and Acceptance
THERE IS A PLACE

Performed by Heidi Magleby Olsen

There is a place where you can always go,
Come with me.
Where it's alright to let your feelings show,
Come with me.
What a pleasant journey, isn't very far.
We can go together, stay right where you are.
And now it's time to start; it's right here in your heart.

There is a place where you can be yourself.
Come with me.
And it's a place where you can free yourself.
Come with me.
And you know it's waiting not so far away,
Need no reservations, we could go today.
Now it's time to start; it's right here in your heart.

And the light shines through each window
And the door is open wide
And each question has an answer
If you'll only look inside.

There is a place where every sorrow ends.
Come with me.
Where every hope and every truth begins,
Come with me.
What a pleasant journey, isn't very far.
We can go together, stay right where you are.
Now it's time to start; it's right here in your heart.

A
NAVY
INVENTION

Charlie invents for the Navy

"The thing we run from is the thing we run to."

A NAVY INVENTION

Fear and insecurity ruled my life for many years; therefore, I had to try twice as hard as the next person to make things work. It took one me to create something and the other me to convince myself that what I did was worth something.

Right after I left home to start school in Boston, my father died suddenly. It was the turning point in my life, an experience I would not like to repeat. The major purpose of my efforts had been to please my father, to win his approval and affection after a lifetime of rejection and abuse. Now, all at once, my reason for pushing myself to excel had disintegrated. I lost my drive; I lost interest in school and football. Then I suffered an injury on a construction job. This injury, combined with my attitude, eventually cost me my scholarship,

I left school—to take care of Mom, I told myself. But that was, at least in part, an excuse. The future seemed to come forward abruptly and stare me right in the face. I was forced to chart a starkly different course for my life, which was going nowhere.

The Birth of a Business

I came to California to start my new career. I actually found a job with a national company, but the job only lasted three days. Company officials gave me a battery of exams to see how I psychologically fit with the company, and I was fired when they determined I wanted to own them. They were right!

So I was on my own. For some reason, I was attracted to an experimental field of plastic and rubber coatings, brand new to the market. I sold pots and pans at night to make a living, but during the day I studied everything I could find about these coatings and their possible applications.

I was introduced to my first opportunity by a friend whose family built minesweepers for the Navy. The Vietnam War was in full swing, and Navy officials were attempting to activate as many ships as they could. They were searching for a way to waterproof the decks of their wooden minesweepers without having to undergo costly deck replacement.

Through my friend, I got an appointment to meet the naval commander in charge of these ships. I drove to the Long Beach Naval Shipyard in a borrowed car. All I had was a sample of material I couldn't even pronounce. I convinced Navy officials to enter a joint venture with me to do the first ship.

I had no money to attempt a joint venture, but that did not stop me. When the meeting was over, the commander requested a business card and asked me the name of my company. At that moment, Butland Chemical was born.

I had no business card, no address (I gave the commander my apartment address), no money, and no chemical plant, but that didn't stop me. Two weeks later, a black Navy car was circling my apartment looking for Butland Chemical. The driver finally left an envelope in the mailbox. The envelope contained a contract, equivalent to $100,000 today, to test my system on the deck of the *USS Esteem*.

DRIVEN BY PASSION

All my fear buttons were activated. I was faced with the biggest challenge of my life, having to figure everything out from square one. Although I had no money, I somehow had to find a way to hire contractors and buy materials to fill this contract and get the work moving.

A friend, who was an accountant, helped me design a business plan, and I made presentations at every liberal bank that would talk to me. But I was unsuccessful in finding a bank to fund my venture. My fears of these looming, almost overwhelming, challenges were great, but I felt that since I had gotten this far with little more than wits, daring, and desire, I could certainly go the distance. My faith and passion were what drove me— and they outweighed the fear.

Navy officials were calling me daily, wanting a starting date, and I was running out of excuses. One day I was waiting in line to draw the last few dollars from my bank account, and I noticed the loan manager was free. The bank was then and still is today one of the largest and most conservative in California. I knew I had little chance of securing a loan, but I had nothing to lose.

I made a brief presentation, showed the loan officer my Navy contract, and stated that if he loaned me the money I needed to complete this ship, I would secure a contract to do the entire Pacific Fleet. He agreed to loan me the money, saying he could not turn down my enthusiasm. I successfully completed the test ship and was awarded a contract to do the entire Pacific Fleet. At the time of this incredible triumph, I was twenty-four years old.

This invaluable experience taught me that it's not how much money you have or how old (or young) you are that matters. What drives your project to fulfillment is how much you believe in it—and yourself.

Precognitive thinking, which I refer to as psychic abortion, prevents most people from achieving their dreams because of the mental blocks they build for themselves. Recognizing that we make our own building blocks enables us to realize that we are the only ones that can take them down. The birth of Butland Chemical perfectly illustrates what a person can do— regardless of age, knowledge, or money—when his belief system is intact.

STINKING THINKING

Certainly I felt fear during this landmark experience in my life, but I faced that fear. Fear is deadly. You can never run away from fear, you only run to it. The Universal Power is unemotional and impartial to decisions that may either empower or shatter your life. Your ego is self-destructive on a conscious level because it attracts the very thing you fear. Fear is not a spiritual entrapment or conspiracy to make you grow. It is self-imposed by "stinking thinking" based on learned behavioral patterns of your life that came from a variety of other sources.

To change things from the fear level to freedom means simply to face fears head-on and discover what they really are: an illusion. It will help free and empower you to realize that this stinking thinking comes from the collective unconsciousness that has permeated your belief system since man's creation— thinking that every man has had to recognize, face, and eventually overcome.

"COME FLY WITH ME"

When I was growing up, I was taught that being unworthy, sinful, stupid, and negative was a normal prescription for childhood development. My parents had learned this from their parents, who learned it from their parents, and so forth down the line.

I had all the trappings from a deep fear generating from this unrealistic belief system. The outer manifestation of these beliefs, as expressed in the physical, controlled my life until I realized I was part of a much bigger infinite world.

I describe this world as a Life Force that knows only unconditional love, without judgments. This inner world I discovered to be powerful and pure, having nothing to do with what I thought I was on the outside. I didn't need to conquer it, I needed only to be part of it. When I chose to be part of it, it became part of me. *All* I had to do to be part of this consciousness was to rise above the world of illusion where I was an uneasy visitor and summon the courage and desire to step into the unknown.

I sensed loneliness, and even a sense of loss, as I moved away from the energy of my tribal thinking into this nondimensional world. Now, however, as I move with this Higher Power, I don't feel alone anymore. I feel the subtlety of energies operating around and within me.

I find that I am now in control of my feelings, able to guide myself through life in this new and deeper way. I can push my energies into the future and get a readout about how I feel concerning a particular situation long before I actually confront or get into it. I feel a loving, powerful presence, with a form I cannot visibly see or touch. I feel it in every vibrating fiber of my soul—a power that seems to be saying, "Welcome home. Come fly with me!"

CHARLIE'S THOUGHTS
ON FEAR AND ACCEPTANCE

If you are not leaning,

no one will ever let you down.

• • •

It took me a long time to unearth my true self

buried beneath my desperate need

for the approval of others.

• • •

Don't wait for someone to show you the way

or you will only see their back.

• • •

If I accept my poor condition, I will remain poor.

Whatever I accept I become.

• • •

No one thing or no one person

can make you feel something

without your permission.

• • •

Being scared is letting go of faith

in who you really are:

an infinite child of All There Is.

• • •

If you are constantly being mistreated,

you're cooperating with the treatment.

I have never been mistreated by others.

They have affected me only to the degree

I have allowed them to

by my own actions

or failure to act.

The world is positive.

It is only my actions that can make it negative.

• • •

Trying provides two excuses:

an excuse for not doing and an excuse for not having.

I am poor so I live in squalor,

or I live in squalor because I am poor.

Two different thoughts that

42

have the same results.
If one clearly states a purpose first
and then acts on it,
one can change the results of the event.

• • •

Angry people are those who are most afraid.
Anger is fear out of control.
It is where illusions overcome us.
Fear is the horse we ride.
Every fear dissipates if faced head-on;
it becomes a false illusion.
Therefore, I fear nothing in my life.

• • •

Validation is a junk word that measures your self-worth
against endorsements of the mass.

• • •

Being right or wrong is not an intrinsic condition,
it is a subjective judgement based
on a personal value system.

• • •

"Deserving" is a measurement of self-evaluation based
on how you measure up to the rest of the world.

• • •

Growth in life is in direct proportion
to spiritual development.

• • •

There is no need to conquer nature,
just a wish to be part of it.

• • •

When talking, ask yourself if you are
trying to prove something or
if you are trying to display yourself.

• • •

Accept the contradictions
of life without resistance.

• • •

If you require someone to change,
you require that person to lie to you.
No one has the right to change anyone
except himself.
This starts when a person
projects something he or she is not.
I am what I am, and what I am is enough.

• • •

In order for you to be natural, you have to remove
any opinion you have of yourself.

• • •

We fear the thing we want the most.
Fear is deadly, good or bad.
If you fear something bad,
you automatically attract the very thing you fear.

• • •

Once you get to the core of who you are,
you realize there's nowhere else to go.

• • •

You never fail with honor,
and you can never succeed by fraud.

• • •

Try to realize that you are perfect
and go from there.

• • •

I can accept, not expect;
therefore, I have no surprises in my life.

• • •

The thing we run from is the thing we run to.
Fear is the biggest illusion we have.
Every fear faced squarely disappears
because it has no reality,
only a false illusion, appearing real.

• • •

Whatever you are trying to avoid
won't go away until you confront it.
There is nothing in life (even life itself)
that can't be confronted.
As soon as it is confronted,
the fear disappears
and you wonder why
you had fear in the first place.

• • •

I like what I am;
what I don't like is what I think I am.

• • •

What you are afraid to do is a clear indicator
of the next thing you need to do.
Fear is a roadblock to peace and joy.
It is also a signpost that can be used

effectively to produce peace.
If I fear something,
it means that I haven't faced the issue
but I know it's there,
almost like being afraid of the dark.
Once light is shed,
it all disappears.

• • •

Events in life have no effect on how we feel.
Only our perceptions control feelings,
thus changing how we feel about the event.

• • •

If your life isn't working the way you want it to,
notice you're lying. We rationalize
our lives to adjust to the artificial imitations
of our lives. We lie to adjust
rather than change the condition.
It is called "circle thinking,"
but I call it "stinking thinking."
When our life is not working,
we become excellent liars.

• • •

When you have no demands,
everything is available to you.

• • •

Always think of the world as an extension
of the environment and never judge it—
just live and accept it.
Growth will come quickly.

• • •

Worry comes from the belief that you are powerless.
Worry is a false emotion appearing real (fear).
It is a total illusion, which when faced,
changes its dimension or disappears.
One feels helpless because he allows
the worry emotion to dominate,
so he feels powerless.
All one has to do is feel powerful
and face the worry issue.

• • •

Money flows toward stability and security.
By displaying doubts and insecurity,
you automatically push your ability and availability
of money away from you.

• • •

Doubt is a junk word that impedes progress.
Never doubt yourself or your abilities.

• • •

You enhance your strength immediately
by becoming detached about judging others
and their behavior. Just become an observer
and you will develop instant strength.

• • •

Most of our lives are about proving something,
either to ourselves or to someone else.
We are always seeking approval
because most of us were invalidated as children.
That is why we always seem to need
to prove something to others.
A sage proves something by doing nothing.

• • •

If you don't start, it's certain you won't arrive.
Most procrastination comes from prejudging
an outcome, which much of the time
prevents people from starting a project.
You can't finish something you don't start.

• • •

What you can't communicate runs your life.
You're as sick as your secrets.
I am struggling with a few secrets,
and I know they are an integral part
of my behavior. I used to have many secrets,
now I have few.

• • •

Criticize the performance, not the performer.
Never judge a person. It's his actions
that may disturb you.
A person is just doing his thing here on earth,
and his actions may be part of his evolution.
The real person behind the action is a soul
that is perfect like yours and mine. We are all here to
experience our evolution.

• • •

What works for you may not work for someone else.
So what makes you think your way is so much better?
We are all in this world together, going separate ways
collectively. My ideas are only good for me.
I can't preach what's good for someone else when I
don't know what they are experiencing.

• • •

The past is past! I have no memory of bad pasts,
just bad illusions.

• • •

Don't judge a person by his relatives.

• • •

I used to have excuses for my past behavioral
problems. I find that the fewer excuses I make,
the fewer problems I have.

• • •

It's okay to have defects and some bad habits.
What isn't okay is to own them,
so you think you are the defect and the problem.

• • •

Most experts won't experiment to find
other solutions because it may prove
that their pet theory is wrong.

• • •

Being scared of something makes it real.
Ironically the individual, craving survival,
attracts its own destruction. I fear Nothing!

• • •

Don't ever resist anything.
If trouble comes, let it flow through you
without judgment and fear.
What you become when it is on the other side
of you will be an illusion
going away from you.

• • •

Anger is caused by a contradiction of something
we have a strong opinion or expectation of.
If we eliminate all expectations by trying
to enforce our points of view, we can destroy anger.

• • •

My key to growth each day is to use
good references about myself, to acknowledge
my good attributes, which are many.
I use these for stepping-stones to victories
for all my future accomplishments,
which will be many.
My past is the key, not the lock.

• • •

Pride to character is like an attic to a house:
the highest part and the most empty.

• • •

52

Compulsion is when you lose control of your ego.
Ego makes a decision, and you feel helpless
not to go along with it.

• • •

The lions will sleep with the sheep—but the sheep
won't get much sleep.

• • •

Fear can help us turn away from hate
to understanding.

• • •

Fear is a stepping-stone to prudence.

• • •

I work to become more of me today
and less of them.

• • •

Whatever I accept is what I become.

• • •

Don't "have to" need anything
or you will be dictated by it.

• • •

If you leave your life to someone else,
you will pick up what they don't want.

• • •

As I recognize that life is only a journey
and not a destination, it becomes easier for me
to accept myself as a possibility
rather than a finished product.
My search is endless, therefore I can never
be a finished product,
but only the future possibility
of someone I want to be.

• • •

Being wrong won't get you in trouble.
Trying to defend it will.

• • •

The person I have feared the most in my life is myself.
Unless I am able to address every facet of my being
squarely in the face, I will be running
from myself the rest of my life, never truly being free.

• • •

Faith and Hope
FISHING THE SKY

Written and performed by Kurt Bestor

Instrumental

FROM RAGS
TO RICHES

Ship coming in to dock

"Faith gives you belief, love gives you desire."

FROM RAGS TO RICHES

My exclusive Navy contract started to garner attention from major companies like DuPont, US Rubber,
W.R. Grace, and others that were trying to develop
similar coating systems. They had money and political
power that outweighed my little company, and I sus-
pected that my lucrative contract would be challenged.
I was right.

Coatings were then being considered for flight
decks of aircraft carriers. At that point, I had the only
coating product with a history. I did not understand the
politics of government contracts. It seemed that
overnight several companies came out with systems
that competed with mine. We conducted a trial test at
the Bremington Naval Ship Yard with all candidate
products. The test consisted of having cars, belonging
to ship yard personnel, run over the test panels with
chains. I flew to Bremington to photograph the results.
My coating was the only one intact. I was elated,
because I thought the best product always wins. I
learned I was wrong. I flew to San Diego Air Pac

Command to show the pictures of the test results and was almost ejected from the office. The decision about which company they would use had probably already been made. I found out later the company selected had a retired Admiral on its board. I had my first real lesson in politics.

Learning the Hard Way

I decided to take my system to the construction industry to use on balconies and walkways, thus creating a more aesthetic surface than plain cement. My coating system gave birth to a whole new industry. I created a multilayered system with a carpet effect, yet it expanded and contracted with deck movement and kept the surface watertight. I left the Navy to cut a new trail in the commercial world.

I'm afraid I spent money faster than it came in, and I was always doing creative accounting to get through the week and pay for help and materials to keep going. The construction industry was accelerating at an unprecedented pace, and I had arrived just in time to capitalize on this boom.

My biggest contract, the one that was going to retire me in style, was *Leisure World* in Laguna Hills, California. Company officials selected my company to apply all the decking to their condominiums for seniors. The contract was worth seven million dollars a year for five years. I lined up the financing to support the project in material and labor, and at thirty years old, I found myself in possession of a contract worth 35 million dollars. My troubles were over!

The contract was executed on a Wednesday, and we were instructed to finish the model by the weekend. I turned the responsibility for this project over to my superintendent, Harry, and I headed off to Palm Springs. Harry was the most creative contractor I had, always coming through when we had to improvise due to lack of funds. Life was good.

I returned that next Sunday and found copies of a telegram from *Leisure World* threatening to cancel our contract unless we commenced work immediately. I called Harry's home and found out that he had been drunk since Wednesday. I had never seen Harry drunk before, so I had no indication that he wouldn't show up for the most important job of our lives.

I called the construction office at *Leisure World* and stated that Harry had the flu, but we were ready to move on the project right away. I was asked to come to the office to meet with them. When I arrived, I saw some of my competition sitting in the lobby and couldn't figure out why. In the office I was immediately told that my contract was officially null and void. Thirty-five million dollars and a guarantee to early retirement were terminated in less than five minutes. I was speechless.

My whole world suddenly crumbled. I had no other business to get into, and all my equipment was repossessed. In a short matter of time, I went from being a potential millionaire to a homeless, careless, moneyless nobody. Everyone I knew avoided me as though I had a transferable disease. Cold, black fear engulfed my soul to a point of hopelessness and despair. I felt paralyzed by this fear. Even today, as I write this story, it is intensely painful to relive these experiences that have crystallized in my memory.

For years I blamed Harry for all that I lost, but in retrospect I realize that it was myself who was the cause, because I didn't take care of business. The ultimate responsibility rested with me; it was I who failed myself and those who were depending on me. I was fortunate that I was a young man. I learned a very expensive lesson that I will never forget, and I had time to pick myself up, look hard at the realities, forgive, put my failure behind me, and start again. I had lost my passion for this business. I knew I had to find something else that could engender my dedication and enthusiasm.

SMELLS FISHY TO ME

It was a challenge, not an opportunity, that called me to the seafood business. The only knowledge I had about seafood was how good it tasted, nothing more.

One of my New England relatives asked me to ascertain if there was a market for East Coast clams in the area. I agreed to do preliminary inquiries about this popular New England seafood with a few L.A. restaurants.

To help the cause, my cousin sent me 50 pounds of East Coast clams to use as samples. I had no delivery truck, so I tucked the clams in the trunk of my 450 SL Mercedes. No clams in the world had this caliber of transportation, a fully loaded luxury car with smelly clams. I was off to explore a new business venture.

The feedback I got was very positive. Many people were interested, and I found out a bit about the seafood market in L.A. Apparently the wholesale seafood industry was monopolized by a Mafia-type company that no one challenged because they didn't want to lose their product. They definitely were receptive to a new supplier, but I had no plans on becoming one.

TAKING ON THE MAFIA

Just out of curiosity, however, I decided to call on

this Mafia-type company, offering to sell my cousin's clams to them. In no uncertain terms, I was told to stay out of the seafood business. "You don't understand the business," I was told, "and you'll never get any seafood products besides your cousin's if you try."

I recognized a challenge when I saw one, and this was one. I immediately felt that I had to prove myself, so I began my plans to take on the Mafia.

First, I contacted a large wholesaler in Boston. Telling them I represented Atlantic Seafood (a fictitious name), I started to order products as if I was a well-established company, one they had wanted to do business with for years. Before they found out the truth, I had placed my first order and was in business.

In order to get their attention, I had to order container loads of products, so my first order was fifty bushels of clams. The clams would arrive the following morning, I was told, and I needed to bring payment in full in the form of a cashier's check.

So I found myself with 50 bushels of East Coast clams arriving by air. I had the clams, but I didn't have the customers, or the storage facility, or the delivery truck. The Mafia would soon be breathing down my neck. With no time to really plan, I found myself acting on instinct, flying by the seat of my pants.

A GUTSY MOVE

First I found a building whose former tenant had been a meat packing company. I contacted the owner of the building and arranged to store the clams there until I could figure out what to do next.

My next move was gutsy. I began contacting the biggest customers of the company that had threatened me earlier. I offered them the clams at a price that undercut my competitors by 25 percent but still made me a small profit.

People placed orders, and I was in business. My competitor was livid. He had enjoyed a monopoly for years, and now someone was moving in on his turf. He hadn't had any competition because most people feared him, including his own customers. He relished the tales people heard about his Mafia connections, which turned out to be false. But the image had worked for him until I came along, that is.

The mob actually did run the waterfront and everything in it. Directly or indirectly, you had to deal with them if you wanted product, and product is the name of the game. In this area you didn't have to worry about selling the product, you had to worry about getting it.

I never had any problems dealing with these people. In fact, I enjoyed them, and they liked and respected me and my work ethics. I wasn't afraid to get smelly, and they respected that. We ordered thousands of pounds of seafood by phone every day. No purchase orders or delivery verifications. It was amazing. Nothing was needed but my good word. They knew you'd pay when you got the product, and if you wanted to walk again, you never considered not paying the bill.

Equally amazing was that what you ordered is what you got. Once you got "in," product flowed in the quantities and quality you needed. They never intentionally shorted you on product.

Within a short time, I became the largest distributor of New England seafood in Southern California. My Mercedes trunk grew into a fleet of seven refrigerated trucks. I was flying thousands of pounds of Maine lobsters into Los Angeles daily, along with other assorted seafood.

The company got so large so quickly that the FBI and DEA decided to investigate, looking for possible Mafia connections. Officials decided I had to be connected with the Mafia in order to experience that kind of growth, but they couldn't prove a thing.

My seafood company was profitable, but it took a physical toll on me. Because we worked with perishables, I worked seven days a week, and I smelled like a tuna most of the time. I paid a dear price socially as well; I was unable to get a date. The only advantage the smell offered was that I never had to wait in a bank line very long.

This business venture was a wonderful success for me. I had started a business from the trunk of a car and turned it into a company that earned the respect of many people. I had learned never to prejudge what you can and cannot do simply because you lack a specific background on a business you choose. Once again I learned that you can do *anything* if you want it badly enough.

But now it was time to throw away my fishy clothes, find a date, and move on to the challenges that lay ahead.

SURVIVALIST THINKING

After a bout of creative spending and unwise investing I left Los Angeles to begin anew in San Francisco. I arrived penniless, carless, and careerless; I was so broke that if topcoats for elephants were a dime a dozen, I couldn't buy underwear for a field mouse. But I refused to let this stop me. Thankfully, I had the good fortune of teaming up with a former girlfriend, who took me in until I could recover.

There was never a doubt, regardless of the situation or how tough things were, that I could rise above it all.

There may be a thousand reasons to fail, but there's not one excuse to. My survival thinking always taught me that while I was not always responsible for falling down, I was always responsible for getting up.

BUILDING A SHIPYARD FROM NOTHING

I met my future partner while I was trying to peddle remnants of my Navy coatings for application on seagoing cargo containers. He ran a small container repair facility and convinced me that there was a great opportunity to open a container repair facility for ships. At the time, there was a major move in the shipping industry to place all cargo in steel containers to reduce rampant pilfering. The containers were leasing and selling faster than they could be produced.

The key to our success was that there were no shipyard facilities to repair, store, and ship these containers, and that's how American Container was founded. My partner was responsible for the mechanical part of the business, and I was in charge of making the business end run—often without money. I called it creative accounting: our tools were often bought at swap meets (where ownership was questionable) and we usually hired only people who brought their own equipment. We did whatever we had to do, and everyone was excited and awed at how my partner and I managed to build this yard out of nothing.

One other facility like ours existed, but it was owned by a large financing company. Well-funded, the facility only handled the needs of its own company and subsidiaries. But what we needed was what they had: money and equipment.

Occasionally we would receive one of their containers in for service, and I always instructed the office to bill them at cost. Not below, not above, just direct cost. My suspicions were that it would not take their accountants long to figure out that it would be cheaper to have their repairs done at our facility, thereby getting out of the repair business. I was right, and soon they went for the bait.

We received a call requesting that we meet with company officials to discuss the possibility of doing all their repairs. On the agenda was also the possibility of us purchasing all their equipment, including paint sheds, welding units, tools of all types, forklifts, and trucks—everything we needed but couldn't afford.

My partner and I met with the company officers to discuss details. As we walked in, I imagine these well-dressed gentlemen took one look at the way we were dressed and our informal attitude and concluded that we'd fallen off the turnip truck. Those conclusions were part of our plan.

We ended up negotiating a deal to buy their equipment if they would lend us the money. We agreed to pay off the loan by repairing their containers; a portion of the cost would be applied to the loan.

We finalized all the details in two meetings. With the stroke of a pen and good strategic planning we not only eliminated our competition, but we also took over their equipment (valued at $300,000) for less than $80,000, which we proceeded to pay by applying a small portion of their repair bill to the loan. We charged them more for the job, so we still made a nice profit. In one fell swoop, we'd tripled our business and furnished the whole yard with new equipment. That's how you build a ship container yard with no money!

Outbidding Toyota

My partner and I were riding high. We had established American Containers as a quality storage container repair facility and had successfully overcome a strike by Teamsters and Longshoremen, earning the respect of the steamship lines we serviced. We decided expansion was next, so we looked toward Oakland. With our cocky attitudes, we felt we could do anything.

We had done so much with so little for so long, we believed we could do anything with nothing.

We negotiated a successful bid with officials from Oakland for some city-owned property. Toyota was also bidding on the land, offering to pay the city a fee for each car the company was able to store. I convinced city officials that we would provide more revenue for them because we could stack containers four layers high, therefore producing four times the revenue. Obviously, you couldn't stack one car on top of another, so we won the lease.

Of course, we didn't tell Oakland officials the whole story. First, we had no business established in the city, and developing that business would take a considerable amount of time and money. Second, sound financial reasoning dictated that expanding our business this early in the game without capital would be economic suicide. It made as much sense as paddling to Hawaii in a canoe. And that's why we did it! My partner possessed an unshakable belief in my optimism, and I felt the same way about his mechanical abilities. We were the Frick and Frack of the waterfront.

We moved a small trailer to this huge nine-acre lot; our makeshift office looked like a Volkswagen parked at the Coliseum. As soon as the phones were connected, I received a phone call from a major container leasing company in New York that had just been awarded the Russian Wheat Deal, a massive contract that called for more than one hundred thousand containers of wheat to be shipped to Russia. This could be the opportunity of a lifetime!

Company officials had heard of us through our San Francisco operation and wanted to know if we had a large enough facility to handle the repair and depot of their thousands of containers. "Of course," I assured them. "We're actually right in the middle of expanding. There should be no problem at all in meeting your requirements." My eternally optimistic mind was working overtime.

The man I spoke to told me he'd be out in ten days to inspect our facilities, and I hung up in a state of shock. I explained to my equally shocked partner that in order to impress our potential clients, we had to have a building to house a paint shed and sandblasting operation plus a yard full of containers. The creative juices started to flow big time; I was in my element.

An Emergency Condition

First, I approached Oakland city officials, meeting

with the head of buildings and facilities. I explained that we needed a building on our lot to accommodate a huge contract, and I spelled out how it could enhance the city's income. I knew this was the only way to get their attention.

This gentleman mentioned that currently the city was tearing down a building at the airport. "You can have that," he said. Our building prayers were answered, and I called my partner and told him the good news. He immediately dispatched a crew and forklift to tear down the building. We had most of the building down (with pieces numbered so we would be able to rebuild it on our lot) when a very disturbed head of buildings and facilities arrived on the scene. He put an immediate stop to the work, noting that we had no permit to tear down the building, let alone move it. To make matters worse, he mentioned that at the time there was a building moratorium, and the chances of us actually obtaining those permits were small.

I went to City Hall and talked to as many people as I could, including representatives from the mayor's office, pleading for a permit under an "emergency condition." Miraculously (we all know how much time it can take to cut through government red tape), key personnel relinquished, and we got our special permit.

While my partner was moving the building, I was convincing an architect to design me a schematic drawing, illustrating how the containers would be ferried through our building on railway tracks to be sandblasted and painted. "I can do that," he agreed. "But it will take weeks."

I told him that I had less than eight days before my clients arrived, and I needed the drawings before that, regardless of what they looked like. He delivered in five days, amazing even himself that he could do it.

We now had our building up, and we were praying for good weather; a big wind would blow our building right over. But it would have to suffice. Now that we had our structure for sandblasting and painting, we took the next step. We contacted a private contractor to set up his operation in the yard for the day to demonstrate state-of-art equipment to our customer as if it were our own.

THE MAGIC OF THE BOTTLE

Now we had three days before our client arrived, but still no containers. We had to fill our yard with containers, showing a flurry of activity. I wanted our clients to see trucks moving in and out, forklifts loading and unloading, sandblasting, painting, welding, repairing, anything and everything. This was show time.

There is a magic on the waterfront, and it's called booze. With a few drinks and my partner's connections, we devised an elaborate plan. We spread the word that if truck drivers would divert their containers to our yard and then drop them off, they could pick up a free bottle at a designated place. Fifteen minutes later, they could pick up their containers. We even hired a uniformed guard to stand at the gate.

The stage was set, except for one blaring problem. Even with the "borrowed" containers, the yard looked empty. We didn't have enough. We decided that we'd come this far with our scheme and there was no reason to back down now. We went all the way. We built a wall of containers four tiers high in a square perimeter with nothing in the middle. When you looked at the lot from the ground, it looked like we had nine acres of containers stored there.

Doomsday

D-Day arrived; the stage was set. We even brought in a couple of temporary secretaries to talk on the phones. (We'd convinced friends to call in periodically, just to make the phones ring.) We had everything covered—except the unexpected conditions of nature.

Our clients arrived, all ten of them. We were shocked; why so many? Apparently, the project was so important that everyone connected to the program wanted to inspect us. But things went well, better even than we'd expected. Once the word about the free bottles got out, eager drivers almost caused a traffic jam getting in and out of the yard.

I showed the schematics our architect had hurriedly drawn, explaining how we were going to motorize the sandblasting and painting to accelerate the process. Everyone seemed reasonably impressed; they stated they were satisfied with what they'd seen. Because they had another meeting, all of them left except for two young guys. We thought they were new to the business and wanted to know more about how our operation worked.

Suddenly, things started falling apart. First, the wind picked up and our makeshift building collapsed. Fortunately, no one was hurt. I explained to the young men that we were in the process of moving the building and had removed some of the foundations. Wanting to get them out of there before anything else fell apart, I suggested we go to lunch.

As we were leaving, we noticed the security guard slumped against the fence, obviously drunk. We drove up the ramp to the freeway, and I glanced back at our lot. Horrified, I realized that when we had built our container fortress, we had neglected to think about the view from the freeway. You could see the empty center from the ramp! Quickly, I diverted our clients' attention by pointing out some fictitious thing on the other side of the car.

The best part of the story came during lunch, when our two friends revealed they were not as new to the business as we had thought. In fact, they were in charge of the container repair operation and had visited our yard earlier, unannounced, to look around as part of their due diligence. We hadn't fooled them one bit, but they were so impressed with our ingenuity, they figured we really could handle at least a large portion of the repairs. We all had a good laugh—and got drunk.

Three weeks later we received our first order, and orders increased from then on. We eventually developed the facility we dreamed of and later sold it to one of the principals from the Granny Goose Potato Chip Company.

I had survived the loss and humiliation, the self-recrimination, the terrors and challenges of starting all over again. With renewed faith and hope, I was able to accept and forgive all the people I had wrongfully blamed, as well as myself for my past failures. I was able to accept my shortcomings as the learning blocks of life—stepping-stones away from self-pity, toward self-reliance, discipline and accountability—turning failure into the highest form of growth and success!

Our One Shot

These are just a few examples of the companies I've created in my life. The process of creating embodies absolute faith and belief in what you are doing. No situation is beyond your grasp, it is only beyond your faith. Faith opens the door to experience, yet we imagine it to be the other way around.

God is often used to illustrate the concept of faith. Many people profess to believe in God, yet they seek a "burning bush" kind of experience to provide absolute proof before they will be convinced. This negates the reality of faith and the power that reality generates inside the soul. Ironically, when we believe in God, or a Higher Power, when we open ourselves to that belief, we have these "burning bush" experiences on a regular basis, without even knowing or recognizing it.

Faith generates hope. Faith enables you to experience an unobstructed view of your objective. This leads to belief, which turns on passion, which ignites creativity! Creativity coupled with action helps you achieve your objective—but without *faith*, the process never starts. When belief is firmly in place, it changes one's concept of reality and allows you the fluidity of ideas that will synergize that concept. Hope will keep this vital, inward condition alive.

I have always had an unshakable faith in anything I undertook, whether it was sports or inventing. My faith raised me above the tentacles of insecurity, low self-esteem, and negativity, that weak legacy bestowed upon me through traditional ignorance. My faith always created a clear view of my objectives. I always knew I could win, regardless of the odds, because of this. The proof of faith and hope together resulted in the creation of world-renowned inventions and businesses—achieved without any formal training and without the skills or background knowledge of what I was undertaking.

I don't think about having faith; I just accept it as a natural part of each of us. Perhaps, because my need was so great, I was willing to grasp faith and hold on tight. I needed something higher and more powerful to direct my impulses and actions than I could find in the world around me. What did I have to lose in giving faith a try? Remember, our life here is not a practice run. It's our one shot; it's the real thing. I think it is exciting as well as empowering to know that with faith and hope, all things we desire and are willing to work for are truly possible!

Charlie's Thoughts
on Faith and Hope

You can't just aim when you are goal setting,
you have to pull the trigger.

• • •

Meditation is a "Windex" to clear the mind.

• • •

Vision is the ability to read a situation
and rise above it.

• • •

There is no right or wrong, only consequences.
It is not the thoughts that count,
it's the actions that follow the thoughts
that will determine the consequence of our beliefs.

• • •

Excuses are your lack of faith in your own power.

• • •

"But" is a lie. It allows one an escape clause.

• • •

*Faith is knowing you have the answer for everything
you are, motivated by your own power within.*

• • •

*An eagle's power comes through his vision,
not his talons.*

• • •

*There is no right way to do something wrong,
and no wrong way to do something right.*

• • •

*It's not the lyrics of life, but the music of hope,
that is the symphony.*

• • •

*Whatever you believe you can do or can't do,
you are right.*

• • •

Faith without action is a good idea going nowhere.

• • •

Consciously or unconsciously,
we always get what we expect.
We create our own reality.
Everyone is going through life
and projecting his or her own reality.
What might seem real isn't and visa versa.
Always be careful what you think
because it can be your reality.
If you don't expect much,
you won't get much.

• • •

There is nothing to fear, only to be understood.

• • •

The strongest people move in silence;
the richest people live in humility.

• • •

It is important to try in life;
what isn't important is how it turns out.

• • •

Faith gives you belief;
love gives you desire.

• • •

Your heart will lead you to freedom;
your head will lead you to bondage.

• • •

There is a universal richness
that has been given to us freely.
We didn't have to qualify to receive it.
Now, through illusion, we think we have to earn it.
How ridiculous.

• • •

There is never such a thing as just good luck,
it is right actions from good thinking.

• • •

It's easier to be negative
because you have more control
due to past behaviors.
To get out of negativity
requires faith to be positive.
In other words, trust and lose control.
That scares people, so they stay in control
at a negative frequency.

• • •

My word has meaning and importance because,
once I give it to myself and others,
it becomes a reality.

• • •

A day has a hundred pockets
when one has much to put in them,
but watch out for the holes.

• • •

Love and Passion
The Melody Within

Performed by Jenell Slack

Music boxes have within
Melodies they carry with them.
Once they open music fills the air.
Every person you have known
Has a song of their own.
Once they open up you'll hear what's there.

It's not easy, you must listen
With your heart for what lies hidden.
There was a melody
Locked deep inside of me, but now it's free,
It found a place embraced by harmony, sweet harmony.

Love, more than anything
Teaches our hearts to sing.
Only love could break the spell,
Now I know very well the love within myself.

LEARNING THE ART OF LOVE

Charlie's Goldens: Broccoli and Zucchini

"Love is the most beautiful verb in the English language. You came from Pure Light, Energy of your Higher Self, safely delivered through tranquility and warmth of a mother's womb. This is pure love."

BROCCOLI AND ZUCCHINI

My early training at home did not teach me any feelings of love for others. My siblings and I simply fell in line with a prejudiced belief system that our parents adopted. Having no experience in respecting those around us or in trusting one another, we could not even love ourselves. It is difficult to imagine, but the word love was never mentioned in our household.

Although my true self has always felt a portion of a Loving Spirit, I never felt a direct connection to it. It was like blocking the center of a bright light: you see fringes of the light around the edges, but you have obscured a direct view of the full intensity of that light.

I always had a passion to find romantic love in my life but never possessed the mental maturity to fulfill that kind of demanding, all-encompassing love. Throughout the years, I had many relationships with some of the most incredible women in the world, yet I couldn't cross the threshold of commitment because of the early belief systems I had incorporated.

I did discover an unconditional love and passion for animals, especially Golden Retrievers. I brought my first two Goldens, Maxwell and Chumbly, into my life when they were ten weeks old. It was instant love, and I soon found myself getting to know a type of parenthood I could not find in the "other" world. These noble animals filled my life, they gave me joy and, like children, some worry and grief.

We lived near the ocean and shared the pleasure of going every day to the beach. It was such a thrill watching these magnificent, free-spirited animals playfully swimming and running through the surf. Somehow, an essential part of myself was living through them. I felt nothing but intense love and joy whenever we were together. Between us, we developed an inseparable bond.

OUR FIRST HUNTING TRIP

I used to hunt birds, and so I taught my dogs to retrieve. They loved to dive in the ocean and fetch a ball or stick and bring it to me. They never seemed to tire and kept returning, their energy unchecked, for me to throw the item out again and again. I experienced so much simple, unhampered satisfaction in watching them frolic in the water. After awhile, I knew it was time to put them to the real test.

We headed off on our first hunting trip, my own anticipation soaring. My girlfriend and I rented a motor home, which we drove up to Oregon where I had some property that bordered a marsh. This was the dogs' first experience in the woods, and they loved it. They rolled on the ground, chewed acorns, and chased each other. What a delight to watch. We had to move our hunting location because the marsh was frozen over. But we were fortunate enough to meet a guide who took us to another area located near a main highway. We loaded the dogs and decoys onto our boat, and I paddled up the river to a more remote area in search of ducks.

My dogs and I sat by the pond. The dogs were very excited, like kids who know something fun is going to happen. In no time at all, I shot two ducks, and the dogs knew instinctively what to do. They brought the birds back to me, trotting proudly, gleaming and shivering with delight. They had finally found out what their training was all about; they had experienced the ultimate reward well-performed. I was so proud of them. It was analogous to something other parents might experience when a son they have loved and worked with hits a home run in Little League.

After this success, I packed up and paddled back to the base camp. We were cold and wet but too excited and happy to care. I couldn't wait to tell my girlfriend how well the dogs had done. She had been witness to the training process, watching them develop and grow.

When we arrived at the camp, I went inside our motor home to get a towel to dry the dogs off. Suddenly I became very fearful about something; a feeling, a strange stillness struck me. Something was wrong. I ran outside, and it was very quiet. I called for my dogs. No response. No sound. Nothing. I looked out toward the road and, to my shock, I saw two yellow bodies lying along the asphalt. In the one instant I had left them, they had run into the highway and been killed.

A RELATIONSHIP BLUEPRINT

Part of me died with my friends that night. It seemed all my childhood pain and suffering was being relived in this terrible night in Oregon. These gentle beasts had taught me the unconditional love and commitment that I was not able to experience in the world of people. And now they were gone. Instantly, irrevocably, what was most precious in my life, that which I had given the most of myself to, had been taken away.

Like everything else, life moves on. God gave me my lesson concerning unconditional love. What was left, after the ashes of my memory of Maxwell and Chumbly were blown away, was the priceless blueprint I could apply to all the relationships in my life, all my encounters with people, personal and impersonal, if I had the courage to try.

During the next ten years, I raised five more Goldens: Broccoli, Zucchini, Rhubarb, Dandelion, and Cauliflower. I treated them with the same passion and love I had learned from my first two dogs. Surely one has to keep giving and giving, I learned, despite the pain. Otherwise, how can life hope to renew itself? I did, however, put my guns away, feeling that I never wanted to hunt again. Another lesson learned, perhaps.

CREATING MY OWN FAMILY

I never had the opportunity for a real family of my own, so I determined to create one. Why not? I could give some child in need a real chance in life, perhaps passing on some of the lessons I had learned on my own. Once I'd decided to create my own family, I went about it in a very unique way, bit by bit, as I came in contact with special individuals.

My daughter, Ensie, for instance, came to take care of my mother who was living with me. Ensie is Swedish for Nancy. When it was necessary for her folks to return to Sweden, I offered to sponsor her so that she could remain in this country. I also kept her as part of my household, which she had already become, finding fulfillment in offering her opportunities and sharing the fabric of my family with her.

Dale is actually the son of a good friend of mine. His father left when Dale was very young, perhaps five years old. I filled the role of father in his adolescent life and am doing so still. It has been a great source of joy for me to be able to offer these young people the unconditional love I never experienced when I was their age.

What is learning and growing worth if we don't share it with others? The circumstances with my other two daughters are much the same, though they did not come into my life until they were teenagers and nearly grown. I have learned and grown from my relationships with them. We travel together; we face crises and struggles and challenges together. They have enriched my life and helped me as much as I have ever helped them.

I still haven't made that depth of commitment to one lady. The fifteen years of life I committed to my mother had a very real impact on me. But hopefully, I will someday experience that consummate challenge and joy. I love and respect the women who have made a deep impact in my life. I can honestly say that every significant relationship I have had in my life is with me still. None of them disintegrated into pettiness, anger, or rejection. Those choice women who took me into their lives are still my friends. Though marriage did not become the end result of any one of my relationships, I have gained much from the kindness and insight of each woman who has held a meaningful place in my life.

A REFLECTION OF YOURSELF

Love is the most beautiful verb in the English language. Love is a four-letter word that can only be felt, not said. Love is not merely an emotion directed toward another person. It *is* everything in life, including the other person.

There are many facets of love. Those facets are directed toward different targets and aims; however, they generate from the same source, a Higher Power who is all love. Anger and hate are generated from a reference point in your learned behavior. We did not come into this world angry; we came from the pure light energy of our higher self, safely delivered through tranquility and the warmth of a mother's womb. This is pure love.

We miss the comfort, sometimes, when life seems to be stopped or going in the wrong direction, but it is always there, and it will never truly leave us. I believe that romantic love is a state of seeing your reflection in another person—the reflection of your Higher Power, embodied in the flesh.

In my formative years, I had no support system that reflected this unconditional love. Love was a word we never talked about. If we experienced love, we almost felt guilty for responding to it or feeling it.

When you cannot touch this love, something you intuitively know is there, it sets up a contradiction to your learned physiological thought patterns. This manifests itself in anger, depression, fear, and negativity. Once you do reach the source or the condition of love, all the cosmic lights come on and darkness disappears. I always knew there was this light. I also know the same light belongs to you as well; it's the birthright of every man and women born into the world. This light shines down on all of us equally. However, we do not all, in turn, reflect the same degree, the same quality, of light.

Love is a mutuality of response. You recognize it; it recognizes you. You don't have to search or pine for it because that thinking always keeps it ahead of you, just out of reach. All you have to know is that it exists in you now, as a power within yourself that you can become. I truly believe that there is a melody locked deep inside each of us. Love is the key that opens the treasure in our hearts, enabling each heart to sing.

Claim the spiritual inheritance that rightly belongs to you through your heart. No words can describe the magnificence of the incandescent light of God. It is in this softness that the human heart is settled. A heart quietly beating, destined otherwise to eventual failure, begging you to expand it further. Help open its powers, that it may carry the torch for others to see: pure love, eternal love.

AN ATTITUDE OF GRATITUDE

Creativity is a metaphor of life. Passion is the fuel of creativity, the force necessary to mold who you are and what you want to be. All my inventions were fueled by an intense passion that anything and everything I attempted could be accomplished. The only restrictions we have in life are in overcoming learned belief systems, which stem from others and deny us of our finest music.

In order to apply your passion, you need to clear the field of anything that has previously restricted you. If you don't perform the basic requirements of clearing, you will be like the cowboy who jumped on his horse and rode in all directions at once. The requirement of clearing is to develop the "attitude of gratitude." When we are grateful for something, we transfer the image to the present.

The Universal Power is all positive, possessing no element of negativity. Only we, as humans, harbor and encourage the negative by *perception*. The Universal Power will give us exactly what we ask for, but it may not be what we had in mind. My early childhood was filled with terror, abuse, shame, and low self-esteem. What saved me was my intense passion to create a reality that would allow me to fit in this world. This passion catapulted me to new heights of creativity that are still with me today. I must be grateful for all the difficult times, because if I condemned them, I would, in truth, be condemning myself. By tasting both ends of the spectrum, I can make a decision. I can formulate a concept, a statement as it were, of what I want to be. Without negative experiences that stretched and challenged me, I wouldn't know the difference—the good from the evil, the light from the dark.

When you transform your *I Wish* to *I Am*, you are working with the two strongest words given to the Universe, because this is a command the Universe understands. Be grateful in advance, as though the condition you are working for already exists. It is a real, living part of you, though you may not see it yet. When you obtain that gut-level clarity, you will feel it vibrating in the deepest part of your soul and know you own it! You can now use your passion to fuel your creativity, to enable you to have anything you desire in life.

Charlie's Thoughts on Love and Passion

If you are going to give a gift,
notice your true intentions.
I always thought there was a payback
for everything you gave.
But if you give something away
it must be given with full understanding
that you receive nothing back,
then your true intention will be known to you.

• • •

To see beauty, you have to leave it alone.

• • •

If you don't like the games people play,
don't play their games.

• • •

I love humanity by letting it become
what it wants to be.

• • •

I love myself by becoming
that which I wish to be.

• • •

Passion is the fuel for creativity.
It is the force to mold thoughts into form.
It changes concept to reality.
Never deny your passion for life
because it defines who you are
and what you want to be.

• • •

The one who loves the least
controls the relationship.
As humans, we always want
something we can't have.
To be attracted by lack of love
reflects where the true lack is.

• • •

All beauty is available to see
when you are ready to look at it.

• • •

Love is a four-letter word
that can only be felt, not said.

• • •

I love this day,
I love what I am,
I love where I'm going,
And I love where I've been.

• • •

The verb love is
the most beautiful verb in the world
if followed by the word others.

• • •

A small action is greater
than the greatest intention
because intention
is not action.

• • •

101

If you are afraid to lose anything you have,

at some point in your life,

you will lose it.

If you love someone or something enough,

you must be willing to lose it to keep it.

If you restrict your love

one way for yourself,

your love can't breathe and it suffocates.

It's the same with possessing anything.

You have to let it go to really own it.

• • •

Feelings are as far away as you think

and as close as you feel.

• • •

You may be one in the world

or all the world to one.

• • •

When you can hold the entire world in your heart,

having love and joy, with no expectations,

you have arrived.

• • •

Love is what love does.

• • •

Feelings are the language of your soul.

Words are the language from your head.

• • •

Joy and Giving
SEA OF TRANQUILITY

Performed by Michael Pedersen

Instrumental

THE
GREGORY PECK
MIRACLE

Charlie and his mother, Mary Butland

"There is no greater joy than the ability
to give it to someone else."

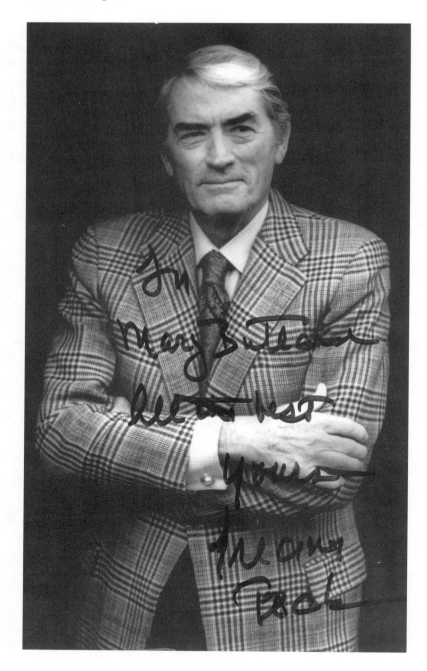

THE GREGORY PECK MIRACLE

Service to others is an outmoded concept today, yet it remains the most necessary element if one is to experience true joy. I gave years of dedicated service in caring for my mother. I cannot say I was joyful for every experience, because there were many times I wished I was doing something else. There were tricky days, but great years!

My mother had this uncanny, subtle way of reaching my guilty button whenever I left her alone. She would give me the look of a kid whose favorite toy has just been taken away, a "go on without me, it's all right, I'll be by myself all alone" look. Whenever I left her, I knew I had to think of something creative that would fill the void and help keep her mind and her spirit occupied.

My mother's favorite actor was Gregory Peck. I had a friend who was an actor who did outstanding impersonations of various people, including Gregory Peck. I talked him into calling my mother whenever she was in a depressed mood and doing a little impersonation of Greg Peck, just for the fun of it. It did wonders for her. She got so excited. "Guess who called me tonight?" she'd ask, then she'd go into every delightful detail of the phone call.

Unfortunately, my friend's profession required him to be paid for his services; after all, it was how he made his living. I couldn't afford to pay him so, out of desperation, I attempted to imitate Gregory Peck myself. I tried it on my speaker phone in my car and was pleased and surprised at how well it worked.

I got five years of good use from that imperson-ation, which enabled me to bring a great deal of joy to someone I loved, a mother who had worked so hard raising us that she never had time to go to the movies or have any kind of social life of her own. Now she had Greg Peck calling her two or three times a week, cheering her up. At the same time, I used the air time to subtly promote how good a son I was, mentioning that I needed to get out more, have more freedom in my work schedule, etc.

Some people may think this was abusive, or at least manipulative, but I never abused my mother. I wanted her to have a life filled with joy, a few simple plea-sures, and hope. And she hoped that Gregory Peck would call every night!

By this time Mom was in her eighties, and her behavior was beginning to revert back to childhood. You could tell her anything, and she would believe you; twenty minutes later, however, she'd forget it. I simply wanted Mom smiling and happy. The phone calls from Greg Peck did both. We had a lot of innocent fun with this fantasy, and it seemed to break the monotony for her. I often wonder if she actually knew what was happening and went along with it to humor me, thinking I needed the help.

A GIFT FROM GREG

As the years wore on, I became more concerned about her loneliness. She did not have hobbies of any sort, and she did not read much. Her day consisted of playing solitaire and watching TV shows. I decided to add some spice to her life, and so I bought her a little pet bird.

I placed the parakeet in a cage and then put the cage outside her door with a note addressed to her from "Greg." She was delighted with her new friend. Mom and Squeaky became inseparable. She would let the bird out during the day, and it followed her everywhere. You could tell where Mom had gone during the day by following the bird trail around the house. Mom was so grateful to Greg for his thoughtful gift.

At the time, I had a hand-held toy that played rude messages when it was activated by a little button. I used to place the toy under the cage and play a message or two. My mother was so amused when the bird would tell me to "drop dead." She always thought it was Squeaky talking; she blamed the construction workers who were working on the building for teaching the bird to say naughty things.

At one point, I happened to meet some people in the movie industry who knew Gregory Peck. Through them I was able to obtain for my mother one of her most valued treasures: an autographed picture of the star. To this day, that picture sits on the mantel in my home. After Mother died, I put a picture of her inside the frame as well, over the much-treasured fan photo. The frame always reminds me of my Gregory Peck phone calls with Mother. Now she's framed together with the fantasy man who gave her so much joy!

After Mom died, I chanced to meet Gregory Peck's son, Tony, and I told him about this game my mother and I had played and the pleasure it had brought her. I gave him a copy of the story, which he passed on to his famous father. Gregory read it and, reported Tony, found it amusing. What a fitting ending to a beautiful story. I wonder what the odds were of this chance meeting that made it possible for Gregory Peck to hear about one of his biggest fans. I wonder if Mother Mary wasn't perhaps cosmically orchestrating something from beyond to pay me back for the years of service I'd given Mother.

TAKING CARE OF MOTHER

I used to take Mom on some of my business trips. I remember one incident in San Francisco when we were staying at a Japanese hotel. I was visiting an office during the day and received a confusing call from my mother. She'd seen the sign that you leave on the hotel door for maid service and was confused. She wondered if she was supposed to make the beds, because the sign she read on the inside of the door read, "Make Up Bed."

This is just one of many stories illustrating our relationship; for fifteen years she delighted and challenged me. Anyone close to us knew the bond we had with each other. I don't think Mom ever knew what I did to get by, to make a living, and she didn't care. There were times I wondered, myself, how I would get by, but I wanted to provide her with some of the good things she had never known during her long, stressful life. I did not want to burden her with my personal problems or the ups and downs of my business affairs. It brought me pleasure to make her happy.

The discipline her presence exacted of me, the extra push of effort I found myself consistently making in order to achieve, had long-reaching effects for good in my life. Perhaps without having had to dig deep, without having to step outside myself in concern for another's needs, I might have been diverted from my goals and sought things that were of less lasting value. Perhaps I would have given into weaknesses and been a different sort of man altogether. Fate pushed me, because I was willing to push and challenge myself, and marvelous opportunities opened up along the way.

My mother was continually teaching me, though she did not realize it. She taught me dignity and unconditional love. She was, by contrast the toughest, softest, most caring woman I ever met. Others were drawn to her and took delight in serving her, in simply being in her company and partaking of her patience, her generosity, her sparkle of interest in other people and in life.

The service I was able to give her brought me real joy, a joy and inner harmony I could never describe in words. I shall always be glad that I did what I could for her. I have been repaid for my efforts during those years many times over in countless ways.

Mom died when she was 90 years old. Young Mary Butland, who cheered others with her courage, her homebaked pies and bread, her patience and self-sacrifice, passed that legacy on to me. Thank heaven I had not been too busy to notice, to care, to take her into my life and be blessed by the virtues and wisdom that might otherwise have passed me by.

After she died, my daughters and I took her ashes back to Massachusetts and buried them next to my father's grave. We also sprinkled a few at the old home where she used to live, carefully carrying them over the ferry to the quiet island that had been her birthplace. A homecoming of sorts, a closing of the circle of one woman's life, a life that encompassed so many others. Who could truly say where her influence began . . . or where it might end?

EMBRACING JOY

During the years spent with my mother, I discovered that giving is the most important linkage to joy, because in giving, one is devoid of ego. When giving, a person is living in a state of real joy within. There is no greater pleasure than in giving to someone else. The spirit yearns to share what it knows, to encourage and lift, to see its light in the eyes of others, shining through the days. Joy is the ultimate experience that permeates all negativity and reflects those pure emotions that are closest to the spirit world.

Joy is what we *are*. Happiness is something we *have*. Joy is the deepest part of our spiritual quest and a natural part of our makeup. We don't have to search for joy, we need only to be it, to embrace it. We do have to search for happiness because it is a behavior connected with earthly activities and pursuits. However, it may not be natural to search. To be natural does not require searching; it does require being in tune with our eternal natures, those elements we brought with us into mortality from a Higher Life, accepting a spiritual heritage that rightly belongs to us.

Joy is not something we have to earn. Rather, it is a harmonious state of being within ourselves. Joy is perpetual; the more we give, the more there is available to us. Finding joy within guarantees joy in everything without. Joy is not next to Godliness, it is Godliness.

CONCEIVE, CREATE, EXPERIENCE

Giving has always been a natural part of my being. When I was a young boy, I worked on a farm six days a week for meager wages. I found real joy and satisfaction in sharing what I earned with my family. It was a natural behavior that is still with me today.

The highest good we can do for ourselves becomes the highest good we give to someone else. The soul is only concerned with what we are being, not what we are doing. There is a distinct difference. The soul is here to learn how to experience joy and love, to produce these desired states so that it may grow. It is this harmonious state of "beingness" the soul seeks, not the transient pleasure of "doing" or "achieving," which is only a reflection of what a person is inside.

My joy today is to draw on all of my experiences and export what I have learned to others, so I might expand their horizons and goals. People who are doing things that are distasteful and devoid of joy are doing them to support a poor misconception of who they think they are.

Conceive, create, experience. New thoughts generate new experiences, and the body begins living in a new reality, and we are able to rediscover ourselves as pure joy. What made our forefathers so strong was not the ability to survive, but the ability to share in a responsibility to ensure that everyone survived!

Joy cannot exist in a selfish state. We need to collectively return to a *we* and *us* philosophy instead of *me* and *I*. There is a terrible loneliness in seeking only self-gratification. Our souls become narrow and hollow if we do not at least attempt to reach beyond our own selves. If you want to achieve something in life, help someone else get what they want. By giving and forgetting ourselves in service to others, we will hear the most beautiful music there is—our own!

CHARLIE'S THOUGHTS
ON JOY AND GIVING

There is brutal and there is honesty.
There is no such thing as brutal honesty.
The most free and rewarding experience in life
is found through truth and joy.
There is nothing forcing us
to receive these gifts.
In fact, they cannot be forcefully given.
They are free of all attachments.

• • •

The art of creating a visible idea
from an invisible thought is the highest form
of the creative process
and can be accomplished by anyone.

• • •

To turn I and you into we is the success
of a full-service life.

• • •

You can get everything in life you want
if you will help enough other people
get what they want.
We are all intrinsically linked to one another.
By being of service to someone,
you get rewarded back through the same linkage.
It's called karma.

• • •

Helping others anonymously is spiritual recycling.

• • •

There is no greater joy than the ability
to give it to someone else.

• • •

If you have to be happy,
you will always be unhappy.
Being happy is a natural emotion
when one has one's life or situation
in a place of comfort.
To force happiness through tools and fools
will never get you there
because you have detoured
from a natural path.

118

Being happy is just being you
and treasuring what you have naturally.

• • •

Dignity is the ability to put someone's needs
in front of your own without judgment.

• • •

The highest honor you can give anyone
is knowledge of yourself.

• • •

Nothing in life works for you
if it doesn't work for someone else first.

• • •

Stability comes from giving, not taking.

• • •.

If you have a constant need to help other people,
notice how you must keep them helpless.
Sometimes we use help for others
in a way that keeps them dependent on us.
This manipulation is another way
to gain control of another,

recognition under the guise
of "just wanting to help."
I need to always look at my motive
when I give something freely.

• • •

Most of the time we don't communicate,
we just take turns talking.
The greatest communicator is the sage.
He talks little but listens to everything.
He realizes he is important
(which makes him so special).
We have to learn from the sage
that the best communicators
are listeners not talkers.

• • •

A cure for shyness is caring for someone else.

• • •

When you face anything in life with truth,
there is a very strange phenomenon that happens.
It's called freedom.

• • •

I choose to have joy today
because I wish to practice
a tool my God gave me—choice.
I can have anything I want
through free choice.
All I have to do is pick it.

• • •

Adversity and Challenges
DON'T LOOK BACK

Performed by Guy Roberts

There was a time when I thought my life was full,
But I didn't like Myself, I didn't know Myself.
They say adversity shows who you really are.

Now that I've been alone,
Felt the pain, I felt all the shame,
Lived with the silence, Lived with the emptiness.

(Chorus)
So I don't look back
(I won't look back).
I know what's right, I fought the fight
The lonely place, Out of the empty space
Parted the sky, Opened my eyes
Now freedom is the horse I ride.

Now that I've found myself,
Now that I love myself,
Thanks to my brothers, to my sons,
And to the friends who inspired me.

Now when I look in the mirror
I see a man that loves,
A man that cares and shares.
This is me. Now I know who I really am!

(Chorus)
And now that I'm complete,
Reached the top of that mountain of life,
And so I celebrate. So I don't look back.

THE
FINGERPRINT
INVENTION

Charlie's fingerprint spray

"Adversity introduces man to himself."

THE FINGERPRINT INVENTION

Some of my most revolutionary inventions involve fingerprinting, the first being a spray utilizing cyanoacrylate, an ingredient in Superglue, that produced latent fingerprints at crime scenes. This chemical was attracted to the amino acids, protein, and salt released through the ridges of a finger when it touched something.

The chemical process developed hard, latent prints that were resistant to smudging—an invention law enforcement officials welcomed and one that paved the way to change the method used for the last 60 years to process fingerprints. Contrary to popular belief, few surfaces produce good fingerprints, and plastic baggies, leather, vinyl, wood, and other rough surfaces are particularly difficult to extract good prints from. With my system, police were able to develop prints from these surfaces.

I developed a small company in San Francisco and started to market these "Superglue Fuming" kits to local law enforcement agencies. My kits stimulated quite an interest. My invention hit the front page of the *San Francisco Examiner* when it was used to develop latent prints on a barrel that held two murder victims. Subsequently, police arrested a suspect, who was later convicted, thanks in large part to my innovative system, which I dubbed Dura-Print.

NATIONAL EXPOSURE

Dura-Print rapidly gained a reputation for its effectiveness in securing prints on surfaces that never before yielded prints. As more and more agencies started to use the system, we started getting reports about prints developed from wet surfaces and dusty surfaces. Police even got prints from a wooden pole used in a murder in Berkeley and from a pillowcase in a Reno rape case.

One day, the producer of *20/20* contacted us, indicating he was interested in filming the Dura-Print process in an actual case, from the initial investigation right up to the trial proceedings. I contacted law enforcement agencies and arranged for their cooperation in letting the public see a behind-the-scenes investigation using this new technology.

The first day the *20/20* film crew arrived in the Bay area, Oakland police reported a homicide. A young girl had been raped and shot. Witnesses identified a car and suspect leaving the crime scene. The suspect was quickly apprehended, and his fingerprints matched fingerprints detected with Dura Print on a wooden table at the murder scene. He was arrested for murder.

At this point, Geraldo Rivera arrived from New York to narrate the story. The whole process from murder to conviction utilizing my invention went down better than a Hollywood script.

WHAT'S THAT AGAIN?

We flew to New York to finish the film at Superglue's Corporate office. Up to this point, I had never met Geraldo; I didn't think it was necessary to meet him as I was only acting as the technical advisor for the story.

But as the crew set up the camera, someone pointed me out to Geraldo, identifying me as the inventor of the system. He asked me to sit next to Superglue's chairman so he could ask me a few questions. I had no idea the cameras were on. I thought we were simply going to chat.

"How did you find your Eureka?" he asked me first. Now years earlier I had had an accident that left me with bad hearing in my left ear. Consequently, what I heard Geraldo ask was "How do you get to Eureka?"

That seemed like a reasonable question since I lived in California, and I thought he wanted to know how to get there. I explained innocently that I usually fly into San Francisco, rent a car, and drive north.

An eerie silence fell over the set, and I was not asked another question. I'm sure Geraldo, the crew, and producers dismissed my answer as typical from a "wacky inventor" and left it at that.

MY FIFTEEN MINUTES OF FAME

We were advised by *20/20* that Barbara Walters was going to host the show and that our feature segment would be the front story.

On July 14, the day the story aired, my house was full of friends as excited as I was about this famous show. Barbara Walters introduced Geraldo, who started off with a story about Archimedes discovering the law of buoyancy in his bathtub. After making the discovery, he ran down the street yelling "Eureka," meaning lucky find.

As I watched, I realized that the cameras must have been on when Geraldo had asked me about Eureka. I became aware that something analogous to the deepest secret I would take to my grave was suddenly going to be exposed to 29 million people. Later, somebody told me that my face turned ash gray, and I looked like a dead person. Frankly, at that point I almost wished I were.

Thankfully, through the miracle of editing, the screen showed me telling Geraldo how to find Eureka, California, but there was no sound. It didn't change anything for me, of course, because I could read my lips. But at least no one else knew my secret. Although the show was a great success and well received, I had to view it a dozen times before I could relax and enjoy my Warholian fifteen minutes of fame.

Although my invention did not have a strong patent and it wasn't long before the process was copied using other chemistry, I was proud of my accomplishment in giving birth to this valuable detection tool. I now had to develop a better mousetrap.

Taking a Chance

My better mousetrap came in the form of developing a Superglue spray can for fingerprint detection, a technology that remains unique to this day.

Unfortunately, I poured everything I had into creating this better mousetrap, and by the time I succeeded, I was broke! This is not unusual with inventors. Most people think you're crazy because of your ideas, then, when you become successful and are making money, people think you're eccentric. Either way, it's a lonely battle.

I designed an attractive ad and placed it on the back cover of *Police Chief Magazine*. I bought the ad on credit, thinking in 30 days I would have enough money to pay for it. The ad was designed to attract a lot of police attention, but mostly, I wanted to attract the attention of a large company that sells to law enforcement. It worked.

Within two weeks, I had a visit from Ivers Lee, a division of the huge Becton Dickerson Corporation. They wanted me to come to their office in New Jersey to discuss my product. They didn't offer to pay for a plane ticket, and I was too embarrassed to ask. Perhaps, if I had not been hard up, I would have broached the subject. But I was well aware of my own circumstances. I didn't want them to come anywhere near realizing that I was broke.

What to do now? One scrambles and takes enormous chances when necessity demands. I convinced a travel agent to front me the tickets with the understanding that I would come back with a check to pay him off. I was such an incredible, naive optimist. I was actually thinking this huge company was going to buy my invention, settle the numerous details, and give me a check—all in one meeting.

A WEEK OF LONG DAYS

I flew to New Jersey and was picked up and taken to the main office where I demonstrated my spray can to the national sales manager, plant manager, and several others. The meeting went well, my demonstrations were successful, the product seemed to please and impress the top executives. But instead of writing me a check, they told me to come back in a week, after they had a chance to evaluate the product—which, in fairness, had literally come out of nowhere. They'd let me know if there was any serious interest.

There I was! I had no money to fly back to California and then return a second time, so I changed the return flight on my ticket and stayed with relatives who, fortunately for me, lived on the East Coast. I paced the floor for a week of very long days, filled with very long hours. I was out of money. I had staked everything I had, and then some, on the outcome of this meeting. I had to return home with a check.

On Thursday, I received a call from company representatives stating that they wanted to see me the following day, the day I was scheduled to fly back to Los Angeles. This was zero hour at its most intense.

When I arrived at the office, I was led into a large room filled with people. In attendance were the company president, comptroller, plant manager, national and regional sales managers, and myself. Again, I demonstrated the product, which made me a little nervous, because it didn't smell good and it made your eyes water. Now, under these tense conditions, I had to sell myself and my invention all over again. I pulled it off with a small spray on a very nervous fingerprint — mine.

The president seemed favorably impressed. He asked me how much my company was worth and, without hesitation, I told him ten million dollars. I have no idea where that figure came from. He asked me to go to the blackboard and give him the figures to substantiate the numbers. I walked slowly to the blackboard, praying for the right numbers to materialize in my mind.

Somehow, I came up with figures that totalled ten million dollars! He then suggested we go to lunch together, and I panicked. All I could think of was how I could get money that day and still catch my flight at 5 o'clock, At lunch, the president offered me a deal that superseded my earlier figures because he had misinterpreted my initial request. I was in a state of shock as he offered me a deal worth millions, as well as consulting fees and expenses. All I could think of was how could I go home with a check.

I stated that his generous offer was less than my expectation, which was far from the truth. However, I continued, if he would secure his offer with a check of $25,000 as a show of good faith, I would agree to the deal. We left our lunch and immediately headed back to the offices, where we worked out a Memorandum of Understanding letter. I believe this was the longest waiting period of my life. I thought at any moment these people would find some glitch that would hold everything up, and I would be right back in the midst of the nightmare again.

FUELED WITH PASSION

The president was going on his own, without the normal committee meetings and formalized steps. I found out later that deals like this usually take months to bring to fruition. But I didn't know that, so I had no reason to think that the nearly impossible could not be done.

Finally, the president, with his house counsel, presented me with a Memorandum of Understanding that mirrored, exactly, our deal. I signed it with a very shaky, sweaty hand, and he handed me a check for $25,000.

The company had a large stretch limousine ready outside to take me to the airport in time to catch my flight. I was able to keep my promise, pay for the ticket, and secure an opportunity of amazing proportions to challenge the days ahead. This proved to me beyond doubt that any adversity can be overcome with enough determination, courage, and faith.

I had also learned that technical or chemical knowledge meant little when developing an idea or product. What really mattered was whether the idea was fueled with passion. I could always hire someone to compensate for my lack of technical or chemical knowledge, but you can't hire the belief and persistence that is essential to make an idea happen.

A COURSE CORRECTION

Adversity introduces man to himself. Life is a creation, not a discovery. We do not live each day to discover what it holds for us. We create its outcome. Adversity is an essential part of the creative process. However, we may not be thinking about creativity when we are experiencing adversity.

For instance, we may suffer a business failure that totally consumes our lives. But, in most cases, what looks like a tragedy turns out to be a correction course to prepare us for something new. An airplane's auto pilot is accurate only ten percent of the time; the remainder of the time it spends correcting itself.

We, as humans, are no different. We are always adjusting our relationships, our work, and ourselves. Perhaps we are only accurate ten percent of the time as well. Therefore, we are constantly faced with challenges and adversities that move us on to the next correction course.

How we meet these challenges will identify ourselves in respect to the most important aspect of our lives: our character. I faced many challenges growing up: the pain of rejection, low self-esteem, negativity, beatings. These were all opposed to my inner belief system, which came instinctively from my own soul. My soul wanted to be happy, joyous, unafraid, and free. I could say that the best part of my childhood is that it is over! It is the same with each and every future challenge that adversity provides. Remember: this, too, shall pass.

CHARLIE'S THOUGHTS
ON ADVERSITY AND CHALLENGES

There are no problems;
there are only dilemmas
that cannot be fixed by linear thinking.
Only paradoxical thinking,
which allows us to work through problems,
gives us the solutions.

• • •

You enhance your strength immediately
by becoming detached about judging others
and their behavior.
Just become an observer
and you will develop instant strength.

• • •

It is not important what one gets from success;
it is what one becomes that counts.

• • •

To be in the spotlight outside,
you have to turn the light on inside.

• • •

You can only have two things in life:
reasons or results.
Reasons don't count.
You have to walk the way you talk
no matter what!
Most people have a lot of motion in their life
but little movement.
I pray my life is full of results
and not reasons why it didn't happen.

• • •

There's no glory getting knocked down,
but there is glory in getting up.

• • •

When making business decisions,
try to imagine that you have over one million dollars
sitting in a bank account.
It allows you to deal with your decisions intelligently
without the influence of your needs.

• • •

Control is like trying to steer a runaway bus
from the rear seat.

• • •

If you are not on the edge in business,
you're taking too much room.

• • •

There are two types of failures:
those who thought and never did
and those who did and never thought.

• • •

If you are not rich,
notice how you make yourself poor.
If you are not perfecting your life daily
to be the person you want to be,
then you are automatically working
in a negative way to be the person
you want to change.

• • •

If you don't like the direction the river is flowing,
don't jump in!

• • •

I can't control the wind in life,
but I can always adjust my sails.

• • •

A mind stretched by new ideas
never regains its original elasticity
if not continually stretched.

• • •

You have done faulty things,
but you are not fault.

• • •

There are no limits,
only restrictive thinking.

• • •

If everyone agrees to the ideas of one,
you have wrong partnership.

• • •

Pride can lead us to a road of humility.

• • •

I have no problem telling people about my defects.
My problem is changing them.

• • •

We never have failures in our lives
if what we have done is to correctly identify
things that don't work.

• • •

Some people are willing to work
only if they can start at the top
and work up,
which means they don't work often.

• • •

Genius is the ability to reduce the complicated
to the simple
and find a way to implement the solution.

• • •

Struggle is a natural observation
of an illusion of life.
Overcoming struggle
is the positive reality of life itself.

• • •

I am my biggest problem
and my best solution.

• • •

If you stick your head in the sand,
one thing is for sure:
you'll get your rear kicked.

• • •

If you look outside, you're chasing struggle;
if you deal with it from inside,
you flow with life.

• • •

Adversity introduces man to himself.

• • •

Procrastination is the ability
to keep up with yesterday.

• • •

In life, pain is inevitable,
but suffering is optional.

• • •

There is no power in darkness,
only in the absence of the light.

• • •

"Well done" is action;
"well said" is laziness.

• • •

Any progress involves risk,
but like baseball,
you can't steal second
without taking your foot off first.

• • •

I can't change the events,
but I can change my attitude,
which overrides the event.

• • •

To reach worthwhile goals,
you don't have to like what I have.
You just have to hate what you have.

• • •

I see many things I have to improve on
and some of the things I need to work on.

• • •

Defects can be used as starting points for change.

• • •

Potholes made me avoid the deep ravines.

• • •

One thousand steps into the unknown
is more valuable than one million steps
into the known.

• • •

Falling apart may be falling together.

• • •

You are not responsible for being down,
but you are responsible for getting up.

• • •

When you lift yourself to the spiritual jet stream,
you find little turbulence.

• • •

The more you let Spirit move freely through you,
the more it sticks to you.

• • •

No rain, no rainbows.

• • •

My life is 2 percent events and 98 percent attitude
toward those events.

• • •

You are only as good as your limitations,
so don't have any.

• • •

There are a thousand reasons to fail,
but there is not one excuse for it.

• • •

Spirit and Womanhood
MEADOW

Performed by Lex de Azevedo

Instrumental

The Legacy
of Womanhood

Mary Wilson Butland, Charlie's mother

"From my own personal standpoint, there is nothing
more confusing, frustrating, fickle, and mysterious as a
woman—and nothing more tender, caring, courageous,
devoted, and loving as that same person."

THE LEGACY OF WOMANHOOD

I have always held women in the highest natural regard. I watched my mother rise above the harsh difficulties of her existence and maintain those essentially feminine qualities of kindness, mercy, and forgiveness. When troubles beset them, women seem able to turn inward and draw on their own resources, thereby increasing the quality and power of that essential "self" that is often marred and misshapen by the pressures and changes of life.

I have had many beautiful, wonderful ladies care for me and teach me throughout my life. When I was young, personal freedom loomed as a big issue for me. Because of the experiences of my childhood, I considered marriage a trap, an institution that robbed and abused human beings rather than enhanced their lives. I wanted to taste as much of the beauty of life as I could, and I knew that much of that beauty would be embodied in a relationship with a woman. But, how was I to achieve that in view of my fears and my own inadequacies?

I remember my first love, whom I was engaged to marry. She taught me the gift of joy and fun. She was always able to keep things light, but she loved passionately. Her spirit seemed capable of finding the light and beauty in all aspects of living, from the humorous to the passionate. At twenty-three, harboring much fear of marriage, I made the painful decision to end the relationship. Today this woman is the proud mother of four children and still as lovely as ever. After that, no one ever met my expectations like she did; my mother adored her as well. She left an invaluable impression upon my soul.

The second woman I came to love taught me what it means to be caring and faithful. At the time, I was in the prime of my life, concentrating on making and spending money, exploring life to its fullest before I "settled down." Today we share a warm relationship, and her family and mine have been close for many years. I am the godfather of her sister's daughter, and I attended her son's college graduation. I am truly grateful for the way her spirit touched and tempered my own.

Next came turbulent years, when I was trying to hold my head above water, progress, put my inner life in order, and care for my mother as well. Those years were not conducive to the establishing of long-term, committed relationships. Yet, during that time another woman I came to love taught me the value and nature of truth. I shall always be grateful for the legacy of truth she left with me.

WORKING MIRACLES

What is it about women? They seem to possess an inherent wisdom, an inner harmony of nature that is often lacking in men. I know that the women in my life have always seen things in me that I could not see in myself. Perhaps women are more tuned to the spiritual. They have faith in that which is not yet formed or functioning. Since faith is a power, they seem able to work miracles in the lives of the people they touch.

Because of my insecurities, my poor training, my fears, and the challenges I chose to embrace, I have never had the opportunity to experience that most intimate relationship between a man and woman, that of husband and wife. I am an explorer; my energies have been funneled in demanding avenues that led me away from this path. Yet I have learned, throughout my life, from women. The most treasured relationships I have to this day are those with women, many which have lasted for thirty years or more. I am grateful for the strength and tenderness that women have bestowed upon me as I have walked life's path.

WHAT WOMEN ARE ABOUT

On my walk, I have observed that there is nothing more confusing, frustrating, fickle, and mysterious than a woman. There is also nothing more tender, caring, courageous, devoted, and loving as that same person.

When we were created, we all had a little bit of woman and a little bit of man in each of us that was shifted to a specific gender by a chromosome transformation. Because of this, I also believe that men have many of the same characteristics as women, except they have been trained not to feel or express them.

Women are different; they feel everything. Women are capable of going with the flow. Men want to control the flow by pushing, pulling, and directing it. Women are able to experience the rhythm and then mold that rhythm to produce harmony. Women see the unseen and feel the untouchable. A woman is capable of hearing the melody of flowers in the wind and seeing the beauty in the unexpressed, even in the unlovely.

At the same time, a woman can be ferocious when it comes to protecting those she loves. Although a woman is not always predictable in lesser matters, she is predictable when it comes to the things that really count, and a pillar of strength when things reach a crisis condition. That's her rallying cry, and she immediately goes into an automatic protective shield position that only a woman would know. Woman can endure more pain than man and complain about it less.

I learned about women and motherhood by taking care of my aging mother for many years. I watched her triumph over every physical and emotional problem with so much grace that I felt miniscule by comparison. She taught me the real meaning of unconditional love.

And, in the final analysis, unconditional love is what women are all about.

During the final years of her life, my mother endured all her suffering in silence. Her only concern was to keep the family together and not to be a source of worry to anybody. I had to do things I found deplorable when she lost control of functions we take for granted, but I realized that we had only switched roles from when I was a child, and she had happily and graciously performed the same kinds of service for me.

Women are graceful *in* their bodies *and* when they leave them. They know when to hold them and when to fold them. They know when to laugh and when to cry.

All these wonderful tentacles of love and complexity are the elements that make up what they love to be called—a woman.

CHARLIE'S THOUGHTS
ON SPIRIT AND WOMANHOOD

You cannot drive a car until you have one;
you have to surrender to a Higher Power
in order to know how to conduct your life.
My own best thinking made me miserable.
I need the control of a Higher Power.

• • •

My spiritual workout is
to exercise my memory of God daily.

• • •

Spirituality is perpetual.
The more you use it, the more is available,
and it grows in proportion to what you take.

• • •

I dedicate my life
to the Higher Power within me.
Through this dedication,

I unfold naturally
to the highest potential of my being.

• • •

Spirit is an energy that exists
beyond scientific knowledge and defies logic
because it can't be defined,
but its presence is found everywhere.

• • •

Independence is directly proportionate
to the willingness to trust and depend
on a Higher Power.

• • •

Material things are illusionary.
Spiritual things are eternal.

• • •

A genius is a person
who recognizes that there is a force
much greater than he is
and allows that force to govern his thoughts.

• • •

You don't find spiritualism,
you live it.

• • •

I always knew I believed in a Higher Power.
What I didn't always know was why.

• • •

There is nothing more confusing, frustrating,
and fickle as a woman.
Yet there is nothing more tender, courageous,
and giving as that same person.
God bless them all.

• • •

Spiritualism is like the sky; it is all around us.
It has infinite depth,
it is colorless,
and you can't touch it,
yet you feel its presence.

• • •

If you have made yourself important,
notice you're not important.
A sage is important

because he realizes that he isn't.
By not thinking of his importance,
he allows the Universal Power
to bring forth his natural abilities
to expand his spirituality.

• • •

Luck is God's way of speaking anonymously.

• • •

I don't welcome hard times,
but I don't fear them either
because I have a new foundation
built on the reality of spiritual connection.

• • •

When you live your life in simplicity,
you are more in tune with the natural state
of who you really are, filled with Spirit.
It doesn't matter what happens on the outside
because the illusion is viewed from within.

• • •

Growth in life is in direct proportion
to spiritual development.

155

There is no need to conquer nature,
only to wish to be a part of it.

• • •

The more dependent you are on a Higher Power,
the more independent you actually are.

• • •

Our attitude toward God is in direct proportion
to the depths of our humility.

• • •

Timetables are human inventions;
there is no "time," only eternity.

• • •

I am God dependent, not co-dependent.

• • •

We live in a relative world.
God lives in an absolute world.

• • •

We are all intrinsically linked together
by a force that created us.

By being in the service of others,
we not only help others,
we help ourselves.

• • •

Authentic power comes
from aligning your personality
with your soul.

• • •

God speaks to me daily.
What I don't do daily is listen.

• • •

Winning and Courage
IN MY MIND

Performed by Windslow Farr

Comin' in from the rain, tired of feelin' the pain,
No lookin' back where I've been,
Hopin' somewhere, someone's there to let me in.

Spinnin' around in my mind
Treasures of life now I hope to find,
All in the grand design
Spinnin' around in my mind.

Comin' in from the cold, no more integrity sold,
Move ahead, don't turn away.
When your heart is pure your soul can face today.

Spinnin' around in my mind
Treasures of life now I recognize
Part of a higher design.
Oh, oh, oh.

There is a book of memories filling each of our lives.
Colors of the sky will paint a sunrise
And freedom will be the crowning grace
Of all who rejoice in the word.

All that I feel inside, spinnin' around in my mind,
Learning the truth of my soul,
Knowing of my Father's love has made me whole.

Spinnin' around in my mind
Treasures of life now I recognize
Part of a higher design
Spinnin' around in my mind.

THE DNA
INVENTION

Charlie receives the prestigious R&D award for DNA

"The way to win is to make it okay to lose."

THE DNA INVENTION

Up to a certain point in my life I experienced many successes, based on my own definition of success, as an inventor. But, from a business standpoint of profitability, many of my past inventions and business ventures were not successful. I can honestly say that I have never failed at anything, but I have recognized many things that didn't work.

The early pioneers of this country fit my definition of what entrepreneurs are all about. They were ordinary people who summoned the courage to cut new trails, facing the unknown and often conquering the seemingly impossible.

Inventors see the invisible, touch the intangible, and create the impossible. We have molded an energy to a form that can be physically seen or touched or known. The clothes and times are different, but the basic elements are still in place. You have to think, do, and move toward your dream.

In 1987, my financial future had never looked brighter. I had patented a new fingerprint technology that was being used worldwide by law enforcement agencies. I had also developed a way of marking art invisibly, with the artist's fingerprint, to prevent forgery. I had a professional board of directors and money in the bank. We were poised to go public and were cleared by the SEC to start trading.

When the stock market crash hit on October 8, 1987, it devastated the company, and everything came to a halt. We had no money to continue along the path we were going, and I was personally responsible for the considerable sum of $350,000 for bridge-loan investors. Viewing the situation with the wisdom of hindsight, I should have declared bankruptcy and moved on to something else. But I chose to stand and fight, just like the early settlers had to do, and they certainly possessed less resources than I.

I next developed a scientific way to find missing children, utilizing fingerprints, voice prints, hair analysis, and video. I developed a "Power Search" program that took effect immediately after the child was reported missing. Facilitated by former FBI agents who were trained in this field, the program was invaluable. Current statutes prevent police from investigating missing persons for seventy-two hours. With the strategy I developed, we were able to fill that gap with my

Kinderguard Program. Unfortunately, my system was not patented and, while I was moving confidently forward, all I had conceived and worked for was stolen by one of my distributors, who bribed most of the skilled people I had trained to join him. I was devastated.

HITTING ROCK BOTTOM

This was one of the darkest periods I can remember in my life. I was caring for my mother full time. I had no funds, no business. The future looked grim, but I refused to quit. I recognized that, no matter what the causes or circumstances, something else had not worked, and it was up to me to move on.

To make things worse, my former partners came into my office on a Sunday afternoon and removed all the furnishings, literally and figuratively stripping things bare, adding additional pain. All my insecurities and low self-esteem came flooding back. Abandonment issues from my childhood reared their ugly heads. I was in serious trouble, but I had to find the strength to keep going. Any other decision would lead to ruination, to literally giving up.

I started to look for a way to make a chemical fingerprint using biological markers. My patent attorney, Sandy Mueller, never stopped believing I would "bring one home" someday; he carried me on his books for years. I will always be grateful to him for not giving up on me.

In 1992, I applied and received a patent for DNA ink that could be used as an antiforgery, anticounterfeit marking. I also applied for a DNA pen and was awarded that patent as well. Counterfeiting was running rampant worldwide, and I knew I could come up with a tool to combat this illegal practice.

By some miracle, I was able to stay in my original office. This was truly a miracle because I had no money to pay the full rent; I was barely making partial payments. But the owners of the building were in as much financial trouble as I was. In fact, while I was a tenant, the building changed ownership three different times.

Every time the building sold, I changed the name of my company and started out fresh. I finally regained some financial footing, refurnished my office, and began forging a new direction for my future. I had overcome the turmoil and injustice of the past and cut an uncharted path through the wilderness around me, just like the settlers did when they came to that first or that second mountain, a mountain they had no idea how they could cross.

My first notable contract was with Hanna/Barbera Studios, a division of Turner Broadcasting at the time. Joe Barbera was the first prominent user of the DNA pen, followed by Mohammed Ali and Joe Namath, to list a few.

In 1995, only seven years after the stock market crash destroyed my life, I was awarded the distinguished R&D Award, dubbed the Nobel Prize for applied research, and recognized as the creator of one of the world's top one hundred inventions. I received the award during a black-tie dinner attended by over 700 people and held at the Chicago Museum of Science and Industry.

Bruce Chapman, a friend and the former chairman of 3M Australia, was in attendance at this milestone evening in my life. At one point, he quipped "R&D (research and development) be damned. It stands for resolve and determination on the part of Charlie Butland."

MY NEW YORK WALLET STORY

With the O.J. Simpson trial, DNA became an international buzz word, and our company became involved in a media frenzy around the world. I was on

every TV program from *Good Morning America* to
Beyond 2000. I was featured in *Forbes, Business Week,
Readers' Digest,* and dozens of other publications. It
was an exciting period of my life. And along with the
excitement came a few amusing stories here and there.

One of my favorites occurred one day when I was
in New York City for business. The Big Apple always
makes me a little nervous. I feel as safe as an alligator
in a purse factory, even though the mayor had recently
assured everyone that the streets of New York were
safe. I agreed with him. The streets were perfectly safe;
it was the people on them that made me nervous!

The day was rainy and gray, and I was late for an
appointment. When it rains in New York, it is easier to
have lunch with the president than to catch a cab. I
found myself in Grand Central Station, waiting in a
long line to get a taxi when a well-dressed, middle-
aged man bumped into me. All of a sudden, I realized
my wallet was missing. That realization was quickly
followed by another: that well-dressed man had it! I
asked the lady behind me, who was reading a newspa-
per, to please save my place. "I'm going to apprehend a
pickpocket!" I explained. She didn't seem too
impressed but indicated she'd save my spot.

NOBODY EVEN CARES

I gave chase to the bandit. He was very nonchalant and wasn't making any hurried attempt to escape. He probably thought he was so smooth that he'd get away with the crime unscathed. Wrong! I chased him down, grabbed his arm, twisted it around his back, and slammed him against the wall, demanding my wallet.

He was very startled that I'd caught him in the act and fumbled around, returning my wallet, which I put in my pocket while still holding his arm. I should have had him arrested, but I was already late for my meeting and decided I couldn't take the time. I let him get away, but at least I had my wallet back.

I returned to the taxi line, where my space was still intact. The lady behind me was still engrossed in her paper, unmoved and uninterested in my recent fight against crime. This only reinforced my insecurities with New York. *Here I am*, I thought, *robbed at 5 o'clock in the evening in Grand Central Station and nobody even cares!*

I finally arrived at my meeting twenty minutes late. When I told the waiting group about my experience with a pickpocket, I was surprised to hear that three of the five people there had been victim of similar encounters. This further reinforced my New York attitude.

Even after the meeting I was still upset. I just couldn't get it out of my mind, continuing to picture it over and over. I had been violated, damn it!

THE REAL THIEF

When I returned to my hotel room, I got the shock of my adult life. There, sitting on my bureau, bigger than life, was my wallet! I slowly reached in my back pocket and removed what turned out to be someone else's wallet. It was I who had mugged someone in Grand Central Station at 5 o'clock in the afternoon!

I looked through the wallet and found a Park Avenue address. It would be the most exclusive area of New York! I was stunned with fear and disbelief. *What do I do now that I am the real thief?* I wondered. Of course, the only thing I could do was return it—anonymously.

After I had wiped the wallet clean of fingerprints, I put it in a package and addressed it. I wrote a note with my right hand (I'm left-handed), stating that taking the wallet had been a terrible mistake. I can well imagine what the owner's reaction would be when he found his wallet intact. I'm sure he figured it had been taken by a non-New Yorker, because it had been returned to him.

The scariest part of this story is that only a few days later I made a presentation at the Fortune 500 CEO conference on anticounterfeiting. In attendance were William Sessions, former director of the FBI, and James Woosley, director of the CIA.

By the time the conference started, I was a wreck. I fully expected the man I had robbed to be in the audience. I could picture him jumping up from his seat, exclaiming, "That's the man who robbed me." I was terrified the entire time.

So it turned out that I was the one New Yorkers should be leery of and not the other way around. I learned a valuable lesson about prejudging places and people. I'm not sure if the man I robbed learned anything!

Currently, the DNA product is used around the world to protect currency, clothing, Olympic 2000 licensed products, and other items. Mark McGwire signed his 70th home run ball at Baseball's Hall of Fame with the DNA pen.

After all the trials and tribulations, the disappointments and challenges, I had finally arrived—arrived by dint of persistence, hard work, and the will to keep going on.

Guaranteed Success

My ability to succeed and continue to succeed despite enormous obstacles and challenges, came from inside. Winning is an inward condition of the spirit more than an outward set of circumstances, prescribed and defined by others, to measure our worth. In order to win, one has to desire something enough to take risks and dare. Failure constitutes a refusal to take that step into the untried, the unknown.

A courageous person is not devoid of fear; instead he has learned how to harness fear, to circumvent and go around it to achieve his best ends. Every time we push ourselves, we hone our judgment and our ability to make good choices. Every time we work hard, giving all we can and then a little more, we develop a greater capacity to work and to perform, at peak level, those things we most want to do.

Blaming others is fruitless and harmful, even when they have initiated difficulties and injustices in our lives. Anger, blame, and self-pity are weakening forces that influence our ability to draw the best from ourselves. By giving in to these influences, we allow those who have wronged us power in our lives, which, in essence, is giving up our own power to grow and change!

Others can stop us temporarily; only we can stop ourselves permanently. If "failure" is used as a stepping-stone to learning, eventual success is guaranteed. Listen only to the voice inside. Use your belief system as a blueprint. Hang on, long after those around you have given up and let go. You will win—and keep winning—because you refuse to accept anything less.

CHARLIE'S THOUGHTS ON WINNING AND COURAGE

You don't have to be positive;
you just have to be yourself.

• • •

It's alright to win all the time.

• • •

Good judgment comes from experiencing
that which came from bad judgment.

• • •

You are the cause of everything
that happens to you.
Be careful what you cause.
I am totally responsible for my life
and its outcome by making right choices.
There are no accidents.

• • •

The biggest risk in life is not risking.
Life is meant as an experience of good and bad.

• • •

Courage is not going against a fearful situation,
it is going in spite of it.

• • •

The secret of all success is hard work.
That's why it's a secret to so many!

• • •

You don't have to be the biggest, brightest person
in the world; you just have to think you are.

• • •

The way to win is to make it okay to lose.

• • •

You win because you refuse to fail.
It's that simple.

• • •

The highest reward you can give yourself is character.

• • •

Others can stop you temporarily,
but only you can do it permanently.
You don't drown by falling in the water.
You drown because you choose to stay there.

• • •

Bondage is false justification for not succeeding.

• • •

What you lack in character
is what you have in character defects.

• • •

An inventor (creator) doesn't reign in
one product or one organization.
He builds products and organizations
so his creativity can flow
and grow through them.

• • •

The only sound winners hear
comes from the sounds inside.

• • •

Your belief system is your blueprint of success.

• • •

Winners know how to win in advance.

• • •

Nothing splendid was ever achieved,
except by those who dared believe
that something inside of them
was superior to the circumstance
and then did something with it.

• • •

One man with courage makes a majority,
because he can gather a crowd in a hurry.

• • •

Success comes from hanging on
after others have let go.

• • •

When you blame others,
you give up your power to change.
Whenever I am angry, jealous, or judgmental
about a person,

I have allowed them to become my Higher Power,
and I become powerless to change.

• • •

Whatever you are willing to put up with
is exactly what you will have.

• • •

It's not product that determines price,
but the energy behind it
that will determine worth.

• • •

A failure could mean success
in a spiritual sense,
but until you stop grieving and let it go,
you'll never know.

• • •

I am the creator of my reality.
Therefore, only I am responsible
for negative or positive responses
to any situation.

• • •

You need to attack life
with so much energy
that you could make a cup of coffee nervous!

• • •

Time is not something you find
when you want to accomplish something.
It's something you make.

• • •

Life and Death
WALKING IN THE AIR

Performed by Heidi Magleby Olsen and Brett Manning

Swooping low over an ocean deep,
Rousing up a mighty soul from his sleep,
We're walking in the air, we're dancing in the midnight sky.

We're walking in the air,
We're floating in a moonlight sky.
The people far below are sleeping as we fly (home).

I'm holding very tight,
I'm riding on the midnight blue.
I'm finding I can fly
So high above with you (home).

Free as we can be
Above the sleeping world.
As far as I can see, all is a dream.

On across the world, the villages go by like dreams,
The rivers and the hills
The forests and the streams.

Children gaze openmouthed,
Taken by surprise.
Nobody down below believes their eyes.

We're surfing in the air,
We're swimming in a frozen sky,
We're drifting over icy mountains floating by.

Free as we can be above the sleeping world
As far as I can see - All is a dream.

TULIPS
OF LIGHT

Last photo taken of Charlie and Mary Butland together

"Life is no more than a paranthesis in eternity."

TULIPS OF LIGHT

One Sunday morning, following a church service, I walked out into a day that was sunny and beautiful. Despite that, I felt an unaccountable self-pity, a depression of spirit I could not explain or understand.

As I stood there, a hidden voice suggested I go to a nearby hospital to visit my friend's wife, who was quite ill. This was a strange impression to come to me, since I had already visited her a few days earlier, and she was to be released to go home early in the coming week. But the impression would not leave me, so I went to the hospital anyway, feeling a bit awkward and strange. When I entered the room and saw her, I knew this would be the last time I would see her alive. We spoke together and visited for a few gentle moments. I was right; she died later that same day.

As I left the building and stood on the hospital steps, I heard the same quiet voice. *Go get some flowers,* it said. I had no idea what I was doing, but I found myself driving to Conroy's Flower Shop. As I stood puzzling on why I was there, a young clerk approached and asked me what I would like.

I looked around a bit and answered, "The tulips look nice." She asked me how many I wanted, and the voice again took over as I responded, "All of them." So there I was, with more than forty tulips in my arms, and no idea in the world what I was going to do with them!

"Is That for Me?"

I started to drive home, and I found myself turning into the parking lot of a local convalescent home. I was feeling particularly nervous, because I had no idea why I was there or what I was doing. *Go inside and pass out the flowers*, the silent voice instructed.

Initially, I thought I'd simply drop the flowers off at the front desk and scram. But when I got to the front desk, no one was there. While I was anticipating my next move, a cranky old lady in a wheelchair, with a cigarette hanging off the side of her mouth, came over and asked, "Is that for me?"

"Of course," I said, handing her a tulip.

As I gave her the flower a most beautiful transformation of pure light came from within myself and surrounded this seemingly ordinary being before me. I did not see a cranky old lady; I saw a pure light being exchanged between us. I could never describe its brilliance. It was something I had never experienced before, but we both knew we had seen into each other's souls.

I moved down the hall and started to hand out flowers to all the ladies. The last tulip went to a lady in the last little room. As the ironies of life would have it, ten years later my mother died in that same room while convalescing on her way home from a hospital stay.

WHAT IS LIFE?

When I left that day, I knew I had no problems, and I could return home in peace. This was a turning point in my spiritual quest, and the effects of it are still with me today.

Those people I had left behind would never go home. And yet, what is it we live for? And what is it we call life?

I had seen beyond their frail, decrepit exteriors, the mortal shell through which we know one another, that temporary house in which the spirit resides. I had seen beyond. I knew Life existed when the physical body was at length laid by. A Higher Power was speaking this assurance to me, reminding me of the true, incorruptible nature of the eternal, which mortal death can neither diminish nor destroy.

To this day, when my kids or I start to feel ungrateful or depressed, we go to the same hospital and pass out flowers to people who find the greatest delight in simply having a visitor. We always come out much happier than when we went in. Hopefully the beautiful souls we left behind are happier too.

LESSONS OF LIFE

With this added insight, I watched my mother gracefully age. As her physical condition and mental faculties diminished, her sweetness became more pronounced. Her frustration melted into softness that swept over her like a warm blanket. She substituted needs for acceptance and allowed little to bother her. Her Higher Power was balancing her for the eventual transformation into a new birth beyond the world of illusion she lived in here.

The spiritual rapture of this sweetness and goodness can overwhelm the human mind with awe. This beautiful creature of God was going home with the grace and dignity she earned. I miss her.

There is little distinction between birth and death; they are only different dimensions. It is only a different dimension we're in. We come into this world as children, and we leave as children. We came to the world in perfect love, free of fear, rigidity, or opinion. We learn these negative traits through the illusion of the world here, which we call life. This life redefines our reality to endorse the preconceived, pre-established orders we find ourselves in. Then, we often spend the rest of life trying to reclaim what was rightfully ours and freely given by our Higher Power—our own true self.

I believe nature is perpetually expanding and, in this process, creating a likeness of itself in the form of human beings. We all came here with a plan for how we were to live, but we are not conscious of this plan because we were placed in a state of amnesia when we arrived. Through free choice, we have the opportunity to explore any dimension of life, in search of our own earth plan.

By overcoming challenges in life, we grow and our knowledge expands. There may be weakness and flaws we have brought with us from a previous existence that we have to overcome, perfections and understandings we need to achieve.

As we age, we gradually drift back toward that cosmic amnesia. We cannot remember things well or keep straight the facts and organizations of the experiences and relationships we have had throughout our lives.

Eventually we remember little at all and dwell largely within the shell of our memories and our own silent, inner selves. This is nature's way of preparing us for the journey home, a wonderful process whereby we revert into children of God in a new dimension.

What I've learned from all my lessons in life is that no matter what the challenges, the common key to survival is love and hope, laced with humor. When you develop humor in your life, it keeps everything simple, and answers come quickly.

Someone asked me once what I would like people to say about me as I lay in state. I replied, "Look, he's still moving."

Charlie's Thoughts
on Life and Death

There are no victims, only volunteers.
We are playing roles for the development
of our evolution here.
There are no sins or bad people.
But there are people doing
bad things in a sinful manner.

• • •

There are many things I want,
but few things I need.
One of the greatest gifts of satisfaction
one can attain
is recognizing the things in life
that are truly necessary
to complete the journey
and the things that are not.

• • •

If you have a college degree you can be absolutely sure
of one thing:
you have a college degree!

• • •

Life doesn't prepare you for anything.
It just is, and that's it.
Once you stop, it stops.
Once you start rolling, it rolls.
Education, like any skill,
allows you to move
in a specific wavelength or energy,
but it is never pulling you.
You still have to push it to work.

• • •

In an information society,
the one with the most accurate information wins.
The one with the most toys still dies.

• • •

A man is what his habits are.

• • •

The world will never value you more
than you value yourself,
but the world will be quick
to reduce your worth.

• • •

It may be true that you only live once,
but if it's done right,
once may be enough.

• • •

An unexamined life may not be worth living,
but an unlived life is not worth examining.

• • •

The best way to double your money
is to fold it over
and put it back in your pocket.

• • •

When you really take a good look at your life,
success is all you've ever had.
If you measure success as getting what you want
consciously and unconsciously,
then we have all had successful lives.

The universe will give you
exactly what you want,
which may not be what you had in mind.

• • •

Thoughts create an integral part of my reality.
Thought coupled with action creates my destiny.

• • •

There are no innocent victims in life.
We are either in our own movies or someone else's.

• • •

When one violates another's rights,
one creates an energy
that restricts one
to the same degree
that the other has been violated.

• • •

You can always tell an inventor,
but not much.

• • •

Most people don't communicate,

they take turns talking.

The best communicator is one who listens

without being critical

or premature with judgment.

• • •

Living is an inside job,

void of outside conditions.

The best things in life aren't things.

• • •

I'm not afraid of dying;

it's living that scares the hell out of me.

• • •

There is no way to know before experiencing.

"You've got to be there," is my favorite saying.

because unless you taste it,

feel it,

and smell it,

it ain't there.

I have had some great experiences

and some not-so-great experiences
in my life.
Those experiences are something
no one can take from me.

• • •

A rainbow is nature's way of exposing its beauty,
but you can only observe it,
you can't hold or touch it.
Life itself is part of that natural beauty
that you can only experience, nothing more.

• • •

You can't create a future
if you always put your past
in front of you.

• • •

Life is a creation, not a discovery.
We do not live each day to discover
what it holds for us.
We create its outcome.

• • •

The nicest thing about life being a play
is that we can be the director
and choose any part we want.

• • •

If you've made it this far in life,
you'll probably make it the rest of the way.

• • •

Money isn't everything,
but it comes in a close second to oxygen.

• • •

Life is exactly what you wanted it to be,
whenever you thought it to be otherwise.

• • •

An artist naturally always signs his own work
because it's a portrait of himself.

• • •

Life is no more than a paranthesis in Eternity.

• • •

The greater the sayings,
the less that is said.

• • •

Life always keeps its agreement with you.

• • •

Everything in nature has a natural bow,
and no matter how you try to pull and twist,
it always gets back to center.

• • •

Loss is an attachment to anyone or anything
that effectively makes you feel
like part of you is gone.

• • •

If you worry about what might be,
and wonder what might have been,
you will ignore what is.

• • •

Before you can break out of prison,
you must first realize you're locked up.

• • •

*If you don't know where you're going in life,
it makes no difference to know where you're at.*

• • •

*A person's life is exactly what he directs it to be:
nothing more, nothing less.*

• • •

You have no life if you have to follow others.

• • •

There have been tricky days but great years.

• • •

*It's alright to have a point of view.
What's destructive is to impose it on others.*

• • •

*Ego is nothing more than a false summary
of what you are,
but you believe anyway.*

• • •

*We spend all our lives searching
for the meaning of our lives*

when it has always been with us.
It's like the absentminded professor
looking for his glasses on his forehead.

• • •

Camelot: a parking lot for camels.

• • •

We came here to learn.
Life is a marathon, not a sprint.

• • •

If you're on a path,
and you know where you're at,
you are on someone else's path.

• • •

When you live by choice, life is a conscious action.
A life of chance is unconscious action.

• • •

Age is relative:
when you're "over the hill,"
you pick up speed.

• • •

Always look for spaces between impulse and action
before engaging the tongue.

• • •

New York cab drivers don't drive their cars;
they aim them.

• • •

Epilogue Song
A Prayer (It Is He)

Performed by Windslow Farr

Ancient Father of my soul
Whose voice is in the wind,
Hallowed be thy name.

From before the dawn of time
When truth became the word
Even the Great I Am.

(Chorus)

See the planets roll upon their wings
As He moves in glorious majesty.
Free your heart and the word fills your soul
Be still and know it is He.

(Chorus)

Free your heart and the word fills your soul
Be still and know it is He.

ABOUT THE AUTHOR

DNA Technologies, Inc. founder and chairman emeritus, Charles Butland, is an internationally renowned inventor/entrepreneur with an impressive history of developing cutting-edge products and technologies. He singlehandedly conceived the idea of incorporating DNA, nature's unique, genetic, building block into ink that could be used to mark virtually any item, thereby creating the first totally foolproof anticounterfeiting device ever invented.

The specialized DNA pen is used by such personalities and athletes as Joe Barbera, Mohammad Ali, and Mark McGwire. Mr. McGwire used the pen to autograph his 70th home run ball in baseball's Hall of Fame. Mr. Butland has also invented a hand-held detector that can be used to instantly verify the authenticity of any item marked by the unique DNA technology. This technology will be used for the 2000 Olympics to protect official licensed products from counterfeiters.

Mr. Butland was honored at the Chicago Museum of Science and Industry, where he was awarded the prestigious R&D award for being one of the world's top-100 technological innovations. The award has been dubbed the Nobel Prize of applied research. He was also nominated for Merrill Lynch, Ernst and Young, and *INC. Magazine*'s Entrepreneur of the Year Award. He has addressed the Stanford School of Business Management and was a featured guest speaker at the 1996 Conference on Intellectual Property together with Mr. William Sessions, former director of the FBI, and Mr. James Woolsey, former director of the CIA.

Mr. Butland has been featured in numerous publications, including *Forbes Magazine, Business Week, Reader's Digest, Wired*, the *Boston Globe,* and *The Los Angeles Times,* as well as on several television shows, including *Good Morning America*, CNN's *Future Watch*, The Discovery Channel's *Beyond 2000*, and *Next Step.*

A New England native, Mr. Butland attended Boston University on a four-year athletic and leadership scholarship. At the age of 24, he founded Butland Chemical, a company responsible for resurfacing all the minesweepers in the United States Pacific Naval Fleet on a priority contract basis. He used an exclusive chemical coating named "Dura-Deck," which he developed during the Vietnam War.

Over the next 25 years, Mr. Butland demonstrated a remarkable talent for taking ideas from the concept stage to development, creating six different ongoing business opportunities. He developed a company to register and search for missing children. The company was based on videos, voice prints, and photographic analysis, and included early search during the first 72 hours before law enforcement search could be implemented. Prior to that, Mr. Butland developed and patented the use of fingerprints and special codes for registration and recovery of lost and stolen personal property.

One notable invention was a Super Glue fuming device that transformed fingerprint technology worldwide. This product, coupled with computers, resulted in the fingerprint conviction rate increasing from 1 percent to 30 percent. Mr. Butland's fingerprint invention was featured on Barbara Walter's *20/20* television show in the 1980s. Though not a fingerprint expert, Mr. Butland created an innovation in the field of fingerprint identification that helped solve the famous Night Stalker serial murder case in Los Angeles and created a new fingerprint technology that is in standard use by law enforcement around the world.

Between 1972 and 1982, Mr. Butland founded three companies that he successfully developed before selling. The American Container Company was a depot, transporter, and repairer of oceangoing containers; the Atlantic Seafood Company was one of the largest distributors and wholesalers of shellfish in the Los Angeles area; and Wintertime Products manufactured combustible logs made by a Butland invention that compressed waste products together into the perfect fireplace fuel.

Mr. Butland also developed a DNA molecular tagging process that can be read by an electronic reader. The information may be coded to reveal distributor networks so as to determine whether a product is genuine and to learn its origin.

Production Credits

Victory in the Night
Written by Michael Pedersen
All instruments, midi sequencing, recording, and mixing:
    Michael Pedersen
Recorded at Stonehaven Studios
Copyright p© 1996 Jade/Tia Music (BMI)

The Prayer of the Children
(Playing time: 4:44)
Written by Kurt Bestor, who also performed all vocals,
    utilizing a vocalizer.
Copyright p© 1992 Riverbreeze Music/The Pinnacle Music
    Group (BMI)

The Boy's Got a Dream
(Playing time 5:10)
Music by Rick Goad
Lyrics by Curt Goad
Performed by Brett Raymond and Heidi Magleby Olsen
Fazioli acoustic piano: Vince Frates
Keys sweetening and arranging: Vince Frates
Drums: Richard "Sneez" Senese
Bass: Craig Poole
Guitar: Michael Pedersen
Vocal backups: Joslyn Petty, Heidi Magleby Olsen, and
Michael Pedersen
Produced by Heidi Magleby Olsen for Signature Music, Inc.
Recording engineer: Blair Sutherland
Mixing engineer: Blair Sutherland and Michael Pedersen
Recorded, mixed, and mastered at Counterpoint Studios, 1999
Copyright © 1992 Goadies Music (ASCAP)

There is a Place
(Playing time: 4:50)
Written by Cinde Borup
Performed by Heidi Magleby Olsen
Fazioli acoustic piano: Vince Frates
Keys sweetening: Vince Frates
Bass: Craig Poole
Guitar: Michael Pedersen
Vocal backups: Heidi Magleby Olsen
Produced by Heidi Magleby Olsen for Signature Music, Inc.
Recording engineer: Blair Sutherland
Mixing engineer: Bob Abeyta
Recorded, mixed, and mastered at Counterpoint Studios, 1999
Copyright © 1994 High Moon Music (BMI)
Used by permission
All Rights Reserved

Fishing the Sky
(Playing time: 4:21)
Written by Kurt Bestor
Piano: Kurt Bestor
Nylon-string guitar: Grant Geissman
Alto and soprano recorders, clarinet: Deron Bradford
Flute: Jane Lyman
Oboe: Brad Smith
Windchimes, finger cymbals, and strings: Brad Dutz
Copyright p©1997 The Pinnacle Music Group (BMI)
Used by permission
All Rights Reserved.

The Melody Within
(Playing time: 2:40)
Music by Kurt Bestor and Sam Cardon
Lyrics by Michael McLean
Performed by Jenell Slack
Fazioli acoustic piano: Vince Frates
Keys sweetening: Vince Frates
Bass: Craig Poole
Guitar: Michael Pedersen

Produced by Heidi Magleby Olsen for Signature Music, Inc.
Vocals recorded at Hudson Forrester Studios, Inc.,
    Minneapolis, Minnesota
Vocal engineer:"Sam"
Music recording engineer: Blair Sutherland
Mixing engineer: Bob Abeyta
Mastered and recorded at Counterpoint Studios, 1999
Copyright © 1996 by Rekab Tserrof, L.C./The Pinnacle Music
    Group (BMI)
Lyrics copyright © 1994 Shining Star Music (ASCAP)
Used by permission
All Rights Reserved

Sea of Tranquility
(Playing time: 3:36)
Written by Michael Pedersen
All instruments and midi sequencing: Michael Pedersen
Drums: Richard "Sneez" Senese
Recorded at Stonehaven Studios
Drums recorded at Counterpoint Studios
Recording and mixing engineers: Blair Sutherland and Michael
    Pedersen
Mixed and mastered at Counterpoint Studios, 1999
Copyright p© 1996 Jade/Tia Music (BMI)
Used by permission
All Rights Reserved

Don't Look Back
(Playing time: 4:01)
Written by Guy Roberts, Michael Pedersen, and Heidi Magleby
    Olsen
Performed by Guy Roberts
Fazioli acoustic piano: Vince Frates
Keys sweetening: Vince Frates
Bass: Craig Poole
Guitar: Michael Pedersen
Drums: Richard "Sneez" Senese
Vocal backups: Joslyn Petty

Produced by Heidi Magleby Olsen and Michael Pedersen for
    Signature Music, Inc.
Recording and mixing engineer: Blair Sutherland
Recorded, mixed, and mastered: Counterpoint Studios, 1999
Copyright © 1999 Tyner/Syd Publishing (BMI)
Used by permission
All Rights Reserved

Meadow
(Playing time: 4:28)
Written by Lex de Azevedo
Piano and synthesizers: Lex de Azevedo
Recording and mixing engineer: Mark Siddoway
Copyright p© 1991
Azevedo Music (ASCAP)
Used by permission
All Rights Reserved

In My Mind
(Playing time: 3:39)
Written by Michael Pedersen and Rick Hancey
Performed by "Windslow Farr" (Heidi Magleby Olsen and
    Michael Pedersen)
All instruments and midi sequencing: Michael Pedersen
Drums: Todd Sorensen
Vocal backups: Heidi Magleby Olsen
Produced by Michael Pedersen and Heidi Magleby Olsen
Recorded at Stonehaven Studios
Mixed and mastered by Barry Gibbons at Platinum Labs
Copyright p© 1996 Jade/Tia Music (BMI)
Used by permission
All Rights Reserved

Walking in the Air
(Playing time: 4:49)
Written by Howard Blake
Performed by Heidi Magleby Olsen, Jenell Slack, and Brett
    Manning

Fazioli acoustic piano: Vince Frates
Keys sweetening and arrangements: Vince Frates
Bass: Craig Poole
Guitar: Michael Pedersen
Drums and percussion: Richard "Sneez" Senese
Vocal backups: Heidi Olsen, Jenell Slack, and Joslyn Petty
English vocals recorded at Hudson Forrester Studios, Inc.
    Minneapolis, Minnesota
English recording engineer: "Sam"
Produced by Heidi Magleby Olsen for Signature Music, Inc.
Recording engineer: Blair Sutherland
Mixing engineer: Bob Abeyta
Recorded, mixed and mastered at Counterpoint Studios, 1999

A Prayer (It is He)
Written by Michael Pedersen
Performed by "Windslow Farr" (Heidi Magleby Olsen and
    Michael Pedersen)
All instruments and midi sequencing performed by
    Michael Pedersen
Produced by Michael Pedersen and Heidi Magleby Olsen
Recorded at Stonehaven Studios
Mixed by Barry Gibbons at Platinum Labs

To obtain order information about this book,
or any other publication
from Signature Publishing, please call
(toll free) 1-888-386-8580
or visit us on the web at
www.signaturepublishing.net